Language and Literacy Series

Dorothy S. Strickland and Celia Genishi, SERIES EDITORS

"Just Playing the Part": Engaging Adolescents in Drama and Literacy
CHRISTOPHER WORTHMAN

The Testing Trap: How State Writing Assessments Control Learning
GEORGE HILLOCKS, JR.

The Administration and Supervision of Reading Programs, THIRD EDITION
SHELLEY B. WEPNER,
DOROTHY S. STRICKLAND, and
JOAN T. FEELEY, Editors

School's Out! Bridging Out-of-School Literacies with Classroom Practice
GLYNDA HULL and
KATHERINE SCHULTZ, Editors

Reading Lives: Working-Class Children and Literacy Learning
DEBORAH HICKS

Inquiry Into Meaning:
An Investigation of Learning to Read, REVISED EDITION
EDWARD CHITTENDEN and
TERRY SALINGER, with ANNE M. BUSSIS

"Why Don't They Learn English?" Separating Fact from Fallacy in the U.S. Language Debate
LUCY TSE

Conversational Borderlands:
Language and Identity in an Alternative Urban High School
BETSY RYMES

Inquiry-Based English Instruction
RICHARD BEACH and JAMIE MYERS

The Best for Our Children:
Critical Perspectives on Literacy for Latino Students
MARÍA DE LA LUZ REYES and
JOHN J. HALCÓN, Editors

Language Crossings: Negotiating the Self in a Multicultural World
KAREN L. OGULNICK, Editor

What Counts as Literacy?
Challenging the School Standard
MARGARET GALLEGO and
SANDRA HOLLINGSWORTH, Editors

Critical Encounters in High School English: Teaching Literary Theory to Adolescents
DEBORAH APPLEMAN

Beginning Reading and Writing
DOROTHY S. STRICKLAND and
LESLEY M. MORROW, Editors

Reading for Meaning: Fostering Comprehension in the Middle Grades
BARBARA M. TAYLOR,
MICHAEL F. GRAVES, and
PAUL van den BROEK, Editors

Writing in the Real World
ANNE BEAUFORT

Young Adult Literature and the New Literary Theories
ANNA O. SOTER

Literacy Matters:
Writing and Reading the Social Self
ROBERT P. YAGELSKI

Building Family Literacy in an Urban Community
RUTH D. HANDEL

Children's Inquiry: Using Language to Make Sense of the World
JUDITH WELLS LINDFORS

Engaged Reading: Processes, Practices, and Policy Implications
JOHN T. GUTHRIE and
DONNA E. ALVERMANN, Editors

Learning to Read:
Beyond Phonics and Whole Language
G. BRIAN THOMPSON and
TOM NICHOLSON, Editors

So Much to Say:
Adolescents, Bilingualism, and ESL in the Secondary School
CHRISTIAN J. FALTIS and
PAULA WOLFE, Editors

Close to Home:
Oral and Literate Practices in a Transnational Mexicano Community
JUAN C. GUERRA

Authorizing Readers: Resistance and Respect in the Teaching of Literature
PETER J. RABINOWITZ and
MICHAEL W. SMITH

On the Brink: Negotiating Literature and Life with Adolescents
SUSAN HYNDS

Life at the Margins: Literacy, Language, and Technology in Everyday Life
JULIET MERRIFIELD, et al.

One Child, Many Worlds: Early Learning in Multicultural Communities
EVE GREGORY, Editor

Literacy for Life:
Adult Learners, New Practices
HANNA ARLENE FINGERET and
CASSANDRA DRENNON

(Continued)

"Just Playing the Part"

ENGAGING ADOLESCENTS IN DRAMA AND LITERACY

CHRISTOPHER WORTHMAN

foreword by
Caroline Heller

Teachers College, Columbia University
New York and London

Published by Teachers College Press, 1234 Amsterdam Avenue, New York, NY 10027

Publisher's note: All chapter opening photographs by Kristine Wolff. Used with permission.

Library of Congress Cataloging-in-Publication Data

Worthman, Christopher.
   "Just playing the part" : engaging adolescents in drama and literacy / Christopher Worthman ; foreword by Caroline Heller.
     p. cm. — (Language and literacy series)
   Includes bibliographical references and index.
    ISBN 0-8077-4246-5 (cloth : alk. paper) — ISBN 0-8077-4245-7 (pbk. : alk. paper)
    1. Drama in education.   2. Language arts.   I. Title.   II. Language and literacy series (New York, N.Y.)
   PN3171 .W67 2002
   371.39′9—dc21   2002020318

ISBN 0-8077-4245-7 (paper)
ISBN 0-8077-4246-5 (cloth)

Printed on acid-free paper

Manufactured in the United States of America

09 08 07 06 05 04 03 02   8 7 6 5 4 3 2 1

*to my son Ryne,
and the teenagers at TeenStreet*

Contents

Foreword

Shortly after you read past this foreword, you will meet Anthony, a young rapper, actor, and painter with TeenStreet, the urban teen theater group to which Christopher Worthman introduces us in this gritty, imaginative, important book. Under the guidance of the company director, Anthony and the other youngsters of TeenStreet are lying on their backs on the floor of a rehearsal stage on a cold winter morning. Their eyes are closed as they engage in the warm-up activity before the dance, music, painting, and writing that typically follows. Christopher Worthman lies on the floor next to Anthony, who, because of his asthma compounded today by a bad cold, breathes heavily and with difficulty. Eyes shut, he takes measure of Anthony's breaths and, "aligning the rising and falling of my chest with his," slowly alters his own breathing rhythm to duet with the movement of Anthony's.

As one might guess from viewing this moment, Christopher Worthman doesn't neatly fit into the generally perceived categories of "educational researcher." Nor does his study neatly fit into the generally received categories of educational research. For more than two years, Worthman was involved in this teen theater company, lending his teaching skills to the work of TeenStreet and entering into the life of the company itself as a participant/observer. TeenStreet aims to foster young people's literacy development and interpersonal understanding through the arts. He began to observe the company, interested in unpacking its educational life and its impact on the literacy, intellectual, and emotional development of the economically poor urban teenagers who participate. A former inner city school teacher, Worthman had already cultivated a deep awareness of the problematic educational life of many inner city youngsters who, for complex reasons, often reject public schools as places in which to learn and grow. In his research, he wanted to better understand the workings of successful out-of-school learning contexts, particularly those successful in reaching disenfranchised young people, like TeenStreet.

While the scholarship of Worthman's study and its potential contribution to the field of literacy education are remarkable in breadth and vision, it is yet another quality of his journey with TeenStreet—a quality harder to articulate, but brought out in his scene with Anthony (and many like it)—which adds to the invaluableness of his book. It is Worthman's openness to the process of research itself that makes me recall anthropologist Clifford Geertz's term, "inner correspondence of spirit." When a study evokes the hope and humanity that Christopher Worthman's study of TeenStreet does while also managing to communicate a research journey so brave and disarming as to inspire a bit of awe, I grasp the truest meaning of Geertz's expression. I came to see that Worthman's quest to earn an inner correspondence of spirit with the youngsters of TeenStreet is not just his way of doing research, it is his way of being in the world. Like the young artists to whom he introduces us, Christopher Worthman is truly onto something, and because of this his book is one of the rare evocations of research that sustains my spirit as well as my intellect.

Caroline Heller

Acknowledgments

I thank TeenStreet for opening its doors to me. It was an altruistic act, and for that and more I am indebted. Ron Bieganski, Anita Evans, and Bryn Magnus warrant my greatest admiration. I thank David Schein and Free Street. Never, I imagine, has a researcher been treated so generously.

This book began as a dissertation, and along the way many people had kind and guiding words to contribute. I thank my dissertation committee: William Schubert, Ann Feldman, William Ayers, Shirley Brice Heath, William Teale, and my dissertation chair, Caroline Heller. Caroline's unswerving support and overwhelming sensibility made this journey easier than it should have been.

I thank my colleagues and friends at the University of Illinois at Chicago who read everything I gave them (which was a lot): Ana Colomb, Steve Mogge, Kate Power, Sue Reynolds, and Cynthia Reyes. We all walked a similar path academically, and their work fueled mine. My appreciation and thanks go to Jennifer Hester, Fran Jordan, Lourdes Kaplan, and Enid Leib for their support, humor, and encouragement. I also thank my colleagues in Bill Ayers's qualitative research class and Caroline Heller's qualitative research writing class for their many supportive and insightful comments on early drafts. Never was I alone in this endeavor.

In going from dissertation to book, I turned to many friends and colleagues for support. I thank Rebecca Kuhlmann at Jane Addams Hull House, Anthony Baker at Ferris State University, Ronald Chennault at DePaul University, and Steve Mogge (again) at Columbia College for reading drafts of the book. I thank Beverly Troiano for helping during the final preparation. I thank Carol Collins at Teachers College Press for her encouragement at every step of the way. Thanks, too, to Michael Greer, development editor, Aureliano Vázquez, Jr., production editor, and to the three anonymous reviewers for their expertise. I appreciate the support and guidance of my colleagues at DePaul University.

The completion of this book would not have been possible without the support of many other people whom I turned to often for respite from the book: Sulaiman Asim, Elizabeth Castro, Ginny Deil, Beatrice Figueroa, Lourdes Kaplan, Jason Lenz, Kate Power, Beverly Troiano, and Judith Velasquez. I thank Ryne and Ampari.

Last, I thank the teenagers of TeenStreet for what they shared with me.

"Just Playing the Part"

1

A Possible World

> Time comes into it
> Say it   Say it
>
> The universe is made of stories,
> not of atoms.
> —Muriel Rukeyser (1978, p. 486,
>   "The Speed of Darkness")

I believe in the part of my head where the top part opens up towards the heavens, growing towards the sun's rays. I believe in the warmth which makes my body tingle in the truth. I believe in that line of melody that pulls that certain something out of my soul, leaving a pleasant ache.

                                  —TeenStreet, MadJoy

My investigation into the creative process at TeenStreet, a community theater ensemble for teens, began with a focus on the ensemble's writing practices. I soon discovered, however, that these were about more than writing, always

1

tied to the movement, improvisation, music, dance, talk, and reading of the teenage participants. To unravel all that—that bundle of interacting creativity—and to get only at the writing would have been to misrepresent the TeenStreet creative process. Thus this book is a critical literacy ethnography written, I hope, in the spirit of the ensemble it presents.

THE ENSEMBLE

TeenStreet rehearsals usually begin with warm-ups and movement activities. On the third Saturday of my first year as participant-observer, however, rehearsal began with a jam session. Everyone—fifteen teenagers and two instructors—was in a circle of chairs in the middle of the stage. Ron, the director, got the session going with a couple of riffs on the harmonica. The teenagers joined in, one at a time, whenever a place opened up. Ty, an ensemble member, followed Ron. He was loud and fast on the drums, leaving everyone to catch up and be as loud as possible.

After everyone was playing, Ron held up a hand, palm down, and waited until he had Ty's attention. He slowly lowered his hand, signaling for Ty to ease up a bit and bring the sound down. Ty nodded, expressionless, his lips tightly closed and eyes nearly shut. He let up on the noise level, but the intensity continued. He appeared to know only one speed, whether he was playing the drums, writing, acting, or carrying on a conversation. Every movement and word from him were punctuated by an exclamation point. He smiled at Ron and held his head up, looking at the rest of the group through raised eyes. His face did not move, nor did his expression change, belying the action of his hands.

The rhythm rolled over the group like a wave, carrying everyone along until each was following Ty's lead. After five minutes or so, Ron asked Bryn, the ensemble writing instructor, to read a couple of poems. Bryn, who had been watching from offstage, moved down to the edge of the stage and flipped to a poem he had marked a few minutes earlier. He began to read and Ron, still playing, stopped him. He told him that his voice should rise above the music like a cork on the water's surface.

Bryn looked at the poem and then at Ron. "What do you mean?" he said.

"The poem is floating on the rhythm, just above the sound," Ron said.

Bryn read louder, trying to be heard over the music. The reading sounded unnatural, as if Bryn were talking over the sound and not above it. The poem he had chosen did not sound right. He finished and shook his head.

Ron nodded and shrugged, then smiled and told everyone to find a place to end. The sound came down and some of the teenagers dropped out. Ty hung on until the end and then stopped.

Bryn looked at Ron and said he was not sure what he was looking for.

Ron continued to smile and smacked a drum in front of him lightly. "I thought we'd try it. I just wanted to see what it sounded like. Just an idea." He looked around at the teenagers, who, like me, appeared to be waiting for something beside the shrugs and smiles Ron was giving them. "Not everything works," Ron said.

Ron pushed his drum away from him. He said he wanted to get back to the idea of "showing off," a concern with which he ended the last rehearsal. The issue had come up during a writing exercise when someone had written a long list of vulgarities to describe someone else.

"People see such language as a source of power," Ron said. "It has shock value. It's being overly violent or sexual or using vulgar language to get attention. It doesn't usually work, because it's boring. We've all heard it before, that's why it is so easy to use. Get away from the same boring clichés," Ron said.

"Why can't we say what we want?" Jared said.

"Say what you want," Ron said. "But that doesn't mean others have to like it or see it as creative. Frankly, it isn't creative at all." He hesitated, then said, "Use your freedom of speech. Use all of it and go the range. Take a chance. Experiment with your freedom. Don't posture and confine your expression."

Nancy said that she was the one who wrote the piece Ron referred to. It was the first time she had written anything like that. She was experimenting with the language: "It was new to me," she said.

"You've heard it before, though," Ron said. "Other than being shocking, does it really say anything?"

"I just don't like you telling me to experiment and then criticizing what I write," Nancy said.

"Well, it's not really the language you used that's the problem," Bryn said, leaning forward. "What you wrote is old hat. It's like buying off the shelf. You go into a store, and you can get the same stuff anyone else can get. It doesn't mean anything. It's lost its meaning because it has become clichéd, superficial, ready-made, and expected. You cut someone off in traffic and they say, 'Fuck you.' So what? That doesn't mean anything anymore to most people. It takes more to get at the essence of your feelings, usually. Why do you feel like you do when you use that language? That's what I want to hear about, read about."

Nancy did not say anything for a moment. "Well, I was experimenting."

"Good," Ron said. "Keep experimenting. Don't expect it to work all the time."

The teenagers moved the chairs offstage and found spots on the floor. Ron walked between them. Four teenagers were absent.

"Shoes, socks, off," Ron said. "Come on, the floor's not cold."

Mona stood in the middle of the floor as the others sat down. She said she is getting over a cold.

"The floor is warm," Ron said, walking past her.

Mona rolled her eyes at Ron and bent down at the waist to untie her shoes.

"I got a cut on my foot," Delphi said. Ron looked at her. She still had her shoes on.

"Okay, I'll get a Band-Aid," Ron said. He went downstairs to the office. Delphi took a deep, loud breath and sat down to take off her shoes.

People were still taking off shoes when Ron came back. He tossed the Band-Aid to Delphi. It died in midflight and she crawled over to it, stretching her body across the floor to reach it with an outstretched arm.

"You got to find excuses to do things," Ron said, "not excuses not to do things."

He sat on the floor in the middle of the teenagers and pulled his socks off, tossing them near the edge of the stage. He lay down. "Okay, everyone on their backs. Feel your back work itself into the floor. Make the floor soft and massage your back and butt into the floor."

THE CITY

Chicago is known for its skyline, but when I look out TeenStreet's third-floor studio window I cannot see any of the images associated with the city. Downtown—the Loop—is less than two miles southeast of the field house, but the windows face west. Looking out, I see the third floor and roof of the three-flat across the street, caught somewhere between renovation and dilapidation. New energy-efficient windows still wear the insignia of their maker and reflect the last strains of sunlight as the sun eases past the building. The roof is strips of green matting running vertically and worn to show outlines of the wood below. Gray smoke billows from the three chimneys as pigeons congregate along the edges and apex of the roof, bouncing and fluttering, never staying more than a few seconds at a time but always returning, anxious.

The rest of the neighborhood is much the same: a mismatch of squat, bent, and bulging two- and three-flats that look as if they've sunk five feet into the ground.

The inhabitants of these homes were once mainly Eastern Europeans—Poles and Lithuanians—but now they are Mexican and Mexican Americans, with a few Whites, Puerto Ricans, and African Americans. The neighborhood is poor and working-class, forever in transition, with people coming and going, starting out or falling back. The Polish names of the park—Pulaski—and nearby Catholic schools—St. Stanislaus Kostra and St. Aloysius—reflect the area's history, while the new public school, Rudy Lozano, is named after a slain Mexican-American political activist.

Small apartment buildings anchor the corners of many blocks. A tall building, maybe thirty floors, looms on the horizon south of the field house. I have been told it is Section 8 housing. Tony, a former TeenStreet member and now the dance instructor, lives there. Behind it are low-income row houses that stretch down to the expressway, to where new $500,000 town homes are being built.

New three-flats—three-story, three-apartment buildings—like sharp-edged, solid toys, seemingly grow overnight in vacant lots around the neighborhood. Young professionals, mainly Whites moving in from the suburbs or more affluent surrounding neighborhoods, buy them. This is a change most neighbors greet with displeasure. Taped to the door of a corner storefront building is a sign that reads, "We shall not be moved. Speculators unwelcome." The neighborhood sits too close to downtown Chicago, criss-crossed by expressways and public transportation train lines and bordered on three sides by upscale, gentrified neighborhoods. A growing hodgepodge of trendy eateries and small art galleries and antique stores mixes with discount furniture and secondhand clothing stores and small ethnic cafes along Milwaukee Avenue and Division Street just south and west of the field house.

I walked these streets every morning after dropping my son off at school two blocks south of the field house. I tried to memorize the names of the stores, but only remember what they sell. I watched a storefront next to a bank be converted to a Pentecostal church, an *iglesia*, the display windows now decorated with religious artifacts. The bank went through its own transformation: a new facade and a new name, stretched across the front, forty feet above the street, in four-foot-tall letters.

Further down the street is a temporary employment agency. Large businesses in the western suburbs send buses every morning to pick up workers at these agencies around the city, particularly in Latino neighborhoods. The buses take them to the suburbs—the industrial parks that are the tax bases of those communities—where they work all day. In the evening, they bus them back to the city, dropping them off in front of the agencies.

The further I moved away from the triangle plaza formed by the intersection of Milwaukee Avenue, Division Street, and Ashland Avenue, the more upscale the shops became. During the two years I was at TeenStreet, I sorted out my understanding of its geography, trying to place it within the larger context that I and the teenagers roamed.

THE SITE

I happened upon TeenStreet one day in 1995 while driving past the Pulaski Park field house to pick up my son at school. A three-by-four-foot sign on the fence outside the door advertised the field house as the ensemble's home. I drove past the sign a couple of times and finally went inside a week later. Kids streamed past, walking home from a nearby school. Some climbed the steps to the field house, where the doors stood propped open. I entered and rode the elevator to the third floor.

The door to one of the two offices was open, and I walked in. A short, lean man with a blond ponytail down to the middle of his back sat facing a computer, his back to the door. The large, high-ceilinged office held five desks, a couple of computers, a long counter by the door with cabinets under it, and the usual office machinery. Books and papers sat piled on desks, and a couple boxes of clothes sat next to a wall. Shelves and cabinets lined two walls. A bike leaned against the wall by a window. The windows, each at least five feet tall, were open. Outside, the fall leaves from the tops of the trees brushed against the field house's brick facade.

I introduced myself to Ron Bieganski, the man at the computer, and he invited me to pull up a chair. He slid his chair back and faced me. I said I was interested in writing and asked if the ensemble did any and, if so, for what purpose. Ron was intent on setting out for me the workings of the ensemble, ignoring my query for a moment to tell me the history of TeenStreet and its parent organization, Free Street. He told me what the ensemble did to prepare a performance, who the teenagers were, and how the ensemble was different from school-based creative arts programs and other teen theater groups. Ron related a recent phone call from an ensemble member now attending Chicago State University whose composition instructor had praised her writing: "Her writing had a rhythm to it that [the instructor] has never seen before," Ron said, "'like jazz,' [the instructor] told her. It's something she said she learned here [at TeenStreet]. Her writing has just really come to life because of her experiences the last couple of years." Ron noted that the performances came from the writing of the teenagers. After a half-hour, he invited me to observe.

THE STAFF

At the time I met him, Ron oversaw most aspects of TeenStreet, including auditions, rehearsals, directing, and production. Physically small, he is strong and agile. His intense gaze, one that can either latch irresistibly onto you or miss you entirely because his thoughts are elsewhere, is rooted in a playful and explorative nature. He describes himself as a wrestler who walked into an art class one day in high school and did not want to leave. Now in his late thirties, his life is an accumulation of creative skills ranging from street performing to oil painting, and jobs from professional percussionist to director and teacher at Free Street and the acclaimed Steppenwolf Theater in Chicago.

Ron was the only TeenStreet instructor I met that first day. Before the first rehearsal a few weeks later, I met David Schein, executive director of Free Street, and Anita Evans, the ensemble's assistant director and Free Street's marketing director. With Ron, she supervises rehearsals, her calm disposition a balm for his intensity. Soft-spoken, she is game for anything. I would later learn that her easy smile lessened the anxiety of rehearsals, particularly in the early goings when everything is new to the teenagers. Like Ron, however, she challenges her creative capabilities and expects teenagers to do the same.

I quickly learned that although TeenStreet activities are similar to activities used by other theatre arts organizations, the creative processes of the ensemble rest with the idiosyncratic styles and sensibilities of Ron, Anita, and Bryn Magnus, the ensemble writing instructor. For most of the teenagers, everything that is done is new to them. TeenStreet's uniqueness resides in how things are done—in its project-based goals—including the relationships of the activities to each other and their purposes and durations. Also unique is how the instructors interact with the teenage participants. Ron, Anita, and Bryn are teachers of unusual ability partly because of what they do, but mostly because of what they encourage teenagers to do.

THE RESEARCHER AND THE RESEARCH

Art historian Barbara Maria Stafford (1997) defines a logocentrist as a person who, "convinced of the superiority of writing or propositional language . . . devalues sensory, affective, and kinetic forms of communication precisely because they often baffle verbal resolution" (p. 23). I entered TeenStreet as a mild logocentrist; my perspective allowed for sensory, affective, and kinetic forms of communications to work in support of writing, but not to the same degree as writing itself.

As a student in school, I struggled and prospered within logocentric environments, which are mainly what schools are. At times I felt comfortable participating in language activities such as whole-class discussion and creative writing assignments. Discussions that could be labeled off-task often brought out a bantering, sardonic self that liked to joke with and challenge teachers. I wrote short stories that teachers read aloud. At other times, I withdrew from discussions and found many writing assignments baffling in both structure and purpose. What little writing I did in school—and I did very little—came back to me marked up, my grammar, spelling, punctuation, and organization not up to par. As a freshman in college, I wrote my way into a remedial writing course with an essay based on a prompt I had misinterpreted.

As I watched Ron and Bryn try to merge a poem with music and then talk about taking risks with writing, I got an inkling of what the TeenStreet creative process was going to do for the teenagers. I had experienced a similar process midway through college. It helped transform my own writing and my beliefs about writing. It was what led me to become a language arts and social studies teacher and then a doctoral student. I wanted the writing the teenagers did to be meaningful, purposeful, and empowering, and while I had always wanted that for myself and my students, I was never quite sure of how to make it so.

THE CREATIVE PROCESS

I learned early on that the working routine of each ensemble is basically the same from year to year. The teenagers rehearse six hours per week, two hours on Thursdays after school and four on Saturdays. Movement, writing, music, voice, and improvisation workshops fill the first four months. From these workshops, an ensemble script is gleaned, made up entirely of the teenagers' writing and incorporating the movement, dance, and music of the rehearsals. The workshops are in the tradition of experimental theater. Performance theorist Richard Schechner (1985) describes the workshop method this way:

> In theater that comes from workshop, there is no preexistent script—or there are too many scripts ("material" or "sources"). The words do not determine everything else but are knitted into a performance text. . . . This kind of work borders on the "human potential movement," a movement that has taken a lot of its technique from theater, dance, and music. . . . When workshops and rehearsals are used together, they constitute a model of the ritual process. Workshops which deconstruct ordinary experience, are like rites of separation and transition while rehearsals, which build up, or construct, new cultural items, are like rites of transition and incorporation. (pp. 20–21)

Simply put, the TeenStreet creative process deconstructs the ordinary lived experiences of the teenage participants and transforms them into "new cultural items," or possible ways of looking at the world. The process is dialogical, with literacy being a tool for dialogue. In many ways, the outcome or script is secondary to the process, to the living out and recreating or reimagining of experiences in collaboration or across media.

The eight-month TeenStreet production process begins in October and ends with a series of performances at Pulaski Fieldhouse in May. The ensemble has traveled to Germany in past summers to perform and participate in theater workshops and a children's theater festival. During the years I was a participant-observer, the productions *MadJoy* and *Body House: A Jazz Tricycle* were performed at Steppenwolf Theater, one of Chicago's noted theaters.

THE STUDY

I started my observations just as a new year-round ensemble began. I soon learned that the year-round ensemble is only one of many programs Free Street offers. There are summer workshops in Park District field houses around the city, performance arts and literacy programs in public and private schools, and clown doctor programs in hospitals. Over the past ten years, Free Street had made youth its primary focus. Some of the members of the year-round ensemble came from summer workshops. Everyone auditioned, even members from the year before who wanted to be in a new ensemble. Ron chose fifteen teenagers. All but three understudies were paid minimum wage to create, rehearse, and perform an ensemble production.

Over time, my interest in the ensemble's literacy practices took on a different focus. Many of the teenagers had had bad experiences with literacy in school but appeared to thrive at TeenStreet. Many voiced a new understanding and appreciation of literacy, particularly of writing. The writing was often subjected to multiple interpretations and revisions, and participants spent a great amount of time looking at and talking about one another's writing. Many of them spoke of their experiences at TeenStreet as transforming their understanding of writing, creativity, and themselves.

Although the descriptions and analyses of TeenStreet that follow hone in on literacy use, I expanded my initial focus on writing to address issues related to literacy development but not often discussed in literacy and composition research and practice. I wanted to investigate what it was about TeenStreet that makes literacy use relevant to teenagers' lives. I also wanted to explore how one might conceptualize TeenStreet's literacy use in practice and in theory, and what TeenStreet can tell us about composition instruction and classroom practices in general. With these issues in mind, I address the following aspects of literacy suggested by the opening vignette of this chapter:

1. The nature and value of a project-based learning environment like TeenStreet's to creativity, literacy use, and human interaction.
2. The nature of dialogical perspective-taking, its limitations and development, and the role of literacy in this perspective-taking.
3. The relationship of the body to language and literacy use, particularly how that relationship influences voice development and the understanding of one's own and others' experiences and perspective-taking.

The teenagers said that the writing done during rehearsals was different from what they were used to doing in school. They were not used to all the discussion and tinkering with writing, or with having others look at and respond to what they wrote. It was a writing process premised on what I came to call *imaginal interaction*, where the experiences of the teenagers' lives were played out visually and somatically and allowed to interact with others' experiences. These enactments fueled the writing, which was itself an interactive process. The process is related to Rosenblatt's (1983) transactional reading theory, where meaning is created in the interaction of text and reader. At TeenStreet, however, the interactions were grounded in dramatic storying—with the imaginative retelling of personal experiences as the text—and in the interpretation of these stories by others using writing, improvisation, movement, drama, and music. Wilhelm (1995) suggests that dramatic storying fosters students' entry into and engagement with texts. He gives reason to believe that the effect may be the same for writing. I suggest here that the interpretation of these stories using multiple mediative means such as writing, improvisation, movement, drama, and music fostered engagement with and empathy for others' experiences, enriching one's own perspective-taking and voice.

Over the course of two years, I observed, participated, and learned with TeenStreet members. The time period included the creation of two ensemble productions from start to end, two groups of teenagers, and about 350 hours of observation. Field notes, audio recordings of rehearsals, formal and informal interviews, writing done during rehearsals, and TeenStreet scripts and artifacts were the genesis for all of the descriptions and analyses presented here. I designed the formal interviews to allow teenagers to reflect on their experiences at TeenStreet, their views of writing and the creative arts both inside and outside of school, and their aspirations beyond TeenStreet. Informal interviews were conversations about specific rehearsal events.

My methods of data collection evolved during my time at TeenStreet. I adhere to the research framework described by Glesne and Peshkin (1992), using qualitative inquiry methods and analysis procedures, including constant comparative methods. Teenage participants and Ron and Anita reviewed interview transcripts and early drafts of these chapters.

Much of what I present has to do with my own experiences and still-changing perspectives about creativity, writing, and what, in my case, it means to be an ethnographer. I like to think my understanding of writing and participant observation did not change so much as it was given definition by what I observed.

THIS BOOK

The chapters that follow present TeenStreet's literacy practices from a critical literacy perspective, meaning that I chose to focus on the transformative or agentive aspects of writing. I chose to explore how literacy use in a multimedia creative arts program influences teenage participants' understanding of themselves and others.

I take my notion of critical literacy from James Gee and colleagues (Gee, Hull, & Lankshear, 1996), who point out that past critical literacy studies have often confined themselves to negative critiques and have failed to offer ideals or agendas for positive change. Although I do not fully agree with this assertion, I do agree that critical literacy proponents need "to develop sociocultural approaches to language and literacy that . . . frame ideal 'possible worlds' . . . " (p. 131). Thus, I venture here a positive representation of a Discourse (capital *D* per Gee) community.

Gee and colleagues define Discourse as "ways of talking, listening, reading, writing, acting, interacting, believing, valuing, and using tools and objects in particular settings and at specific times, so as to display or to recognize a particular social entity" (p. 10). TeenStreet positions its members through the use of a project-based environment to identify and critique commonly accepted beliefs about literacy, creativity, human agency, and human interaction.

Literacy is often other than what it has been packaged to be. Presented as a "gift" given to us in school, literacy "has been used, in age after age, to solidify the social hierarchy, empower elites, and ensure that people lower on the hierarchy accept the values, norms, and beliefs of the elites, even when it is not in their self-interest (or 'class interest') to do so" (Gee et al., 1996, p. 40). While these conceptions of literacy and schooling are being challenged today, the "gift of literacy" has, for the most part, stayed the same. What has changed is the packaging of the gift. Chapter 4 explores the literacy scholarship that underlies this contention. TeenStreet, I argue, offers a different way of understanding literacy, one grounded in each participant's physicality or place and time in the world. I also formulate a way of understanding consciousness that posits intuition, self-reflection, and dialogue as significant to meaning-making and human agency.

Although I frame this as a literacy study, I also see the need to step further into theoretical discussions about human relations. I speak of how we treat one another as human beings and why focusing on a particular way of interacting is important to literacy learning, specifically as it relates to perspective-taking and making sense of experience. Chapters 3, 4, and 5 explore the underlying "ought" of literacy use and perspective-taking at TeenStreet. Chapter 3 builds on Chapter 2 to describe TeenStreet activities and the interaction these activities foster, and my own grappling to make sense of what I experienced. In Chapter 5, I develop my concept of imaginal interaction in an analysis of the movement and improvisation exercises.

Chapter 6 conceptualizes the nature and goal of writing done at Teen-

Street within a selective framework of composition research. I set out the significance of voice exercises in developing communicative voice that arises from one's own time and place—one's own perspective—and speaks to others by drawing on others' voices. I suggest that composition instruction in schools would do well to focus on voice development as it relates to dramatic storying and perspective-taking. Chapter 7 offers what I see as the effects of the Teen-Street creative process on the teenagers, relying primarily on what the teenagers themselves told me.

THE PLAYERS

The teenagers' writing reproduced here is presented as it was written. I have made only small changes, such as spelling corrections, to avoid misreadings. Since I was at TeenStreet for two years, I got to know two groups of teenagers. Although I came to know some better than others, I introduce all of the teenagers here along with the ensemble(s) of which they were members (first or second year) and the roles and creative skills they assigned themselves. All the names, except for the instructors', are pseudonyms.

STAFF

Ron Bieganski	1st; 2nd	Director; instructor
David Schein	1st; 2nd	Free Street executive director; instructor
Anita Evans	1st; 2nd	Assistant director; instructor
Bryn Magnus	1st; 2nd	Writing instructor
Mars Williams	2nd	Music instructor

ENSEMBLE MEMBERS

Anthony	2nd	Rapper; actor; painter
Ty	1st	Percussionist; rapper
Nancy	1st	Singer
Mona	1st; 2nd	Dancer; writer
Elena	1st; 2nd	Dancer; writer
Jim	1st	Violinist
Donna	1st; 2nd	Actor; writer
Denise	2nd	Dancer
Chau	2nd	Actor
Terri	1st; 2nd	Flutist; dancer
Sharon	2nd	Writer; actor
Yusuf	2nd	Rapper; trombonist; actor

Tonya	2nd	Singer
Nick	2nd	Percussionist
Karen	1st; 2nd	Violinist
Charles	2nd	Bassist
Se	1st	Writer
Tony	1st; 2nd	Dancer; actor; instructor
Lisa	1st	Writer; dancer; actor
Bonnie	1st	Violinist
Brad	1st	Writer; actor
Michelle	1st	Actor; dancer
Jared	1st	Actor
Cheryl	1st	Writer
Delphi	1st	Writer
Sheila	2nd	Writer

2

The Boundaries of Our Beliefs

11:00 A.M., SATURDAY, JANUARY 11, YEAR TWO

It is a Saturday morning in January, and outside the sun is shining, a harsh, almost blinding brightness; but it's cold, maybe 20 degrees, and windy, which makes it feel much colder, both inside and out. The wind whistles through the crack under the door that leads to the fire escape and rattles the glass in the windows. Only one of the five black-painted radiators works, and it is too hot to touch. The room is a stage with a heavily lacquered and polished wooden floor speckled with damp mop strands. The teenagers are lying on their backs on the floor, eyes closed. Also on the floor are Ron, Anita, and I.

On the Floor

I hone in on Anthony, the teenager lying next to me, timing the rising and falling of my chest with his so that I can hear him exhale. His is a raspy gurgle of a breath, with intermittent sniffing. He takes a deep breath, and I imagine the air being sucked into his lungs. I take in air and purse my lips to exhale, doing so slowly to feel my lungs gradually shrink like balloons being freed of oxygen.

Anthony is asthmatic and has been fighting a cold for a week. Before and after rehearsals and during breaks, he dances and raps, making lyrics up on the spot or reworking ones he heard before. His short, wiry body is always moving. Words unwind from his tongue like marbles falling one after another from his mouth. He is not smooth but full of force, gyrating. He, too, knows this about himself, writing during a rehearsal in November that " . . . despite all my flaws I'm pretty damn spunky," and later telling me, "I have a lot of energy to vent, like, you know, like, there's no other way for me to get it out. . . . I have these weird things going on in my head and I got to get it out." I'm always surprised when I see him walk across the floor after a brief movement exercise, socks dangling on his feet and shoulders rolled forward, and sit, pulling his inhaler from a bag, needing to take more into himself than he has let out.

Sitting down to write is difficult for Anthony. He can't sit still. Early in the year, he barely got anything down on paper, usually a few lines that came in a flurry, between periods of staring into space and shifting positions on the floor. In November he reflected on a just completed movement exercise, writing: "Alone watching, waiting not impatient yet with a knowing that whatever it is will come sometime, anytime, till then playing out my part in the daily routine of the world, still waiting for whatever I am waiting for." This description came quickly, as if he had realized and pondered it for a while before writing. He wrote quickly and stopped, decidedly finished as others continued. Even the rhythm of his words reflects the movement of Anthony's body, shifting directions, abrupt and forceful, always intense, always purposeful.

Words come too fast for Anthony. He says he doesn't like to write, especially in complete sentences, because he cannot get the words on paper fast enough. "I write and I look back and it's like an alien language, like no periods in my language, no commas. . . . It was always harder for me to write than it was to draw," he says.

Anthony lives with a friend a few blocks from the field house, wanting to be an actor and spending his free time drawing, painting, and taking acting lessons. A month after rehearsals started, he quit his job as a clerk in an art supply shop because his boss would not let him off for TeenStreet rehearsals. More than anyone else in the ensemble, he talks about what TeenStreet is going to do for him professionally. Maybe because he is out of school, he, more than others, looks to the future. I listen to his breathing, thinking he should be home in bed.

More than Writing

It took me a long time to become comfortable in the role of participant in participant-observer. It took me a long time to get on the floor with the teenagers. I am not surprised when they tell me how hard it was for them to participate in the movement and writing activities at first and how they are nothing like anything they had experienced before. Even those with theater backgrounds tell me this. The writing, too, they say, is a far cry from the type of writing they are used to.

Literacy is not something the teenagers give much thought to; it is not something they dissect from other parts of their lives. This is not a reading or writing classroom. Yet literacy is an essential aspect of many of the participants' lives, so much so that although they may find it hard to talk about literacy as an entity unto itself and often describe their school writing experiences negatively, they provide evidence of not only how literacy can play a significant part in people's lives, but also how it is only one part and one possible means of expression, and is invariably and reciprocally tied to others. It is on this evidence, particularly as it does relate to the living of one's life, that I began to reflect during my first year at TeenStreet.

For example, when Anthony tells me he has no interest in writing, I realize that does not mean he lacks for means of creative expression. He is not a writer, so he tells me. His short, powerful descriptions make me think otherwise. But he is an artist and actor, expressing his understanding of the world in ways other than through writing. Yet he speaks confidently of what he has learned about writing, weaving its use into other forms of creative expression. Of TeenStreet writing, he says: "I see this as a very different type of writing. For one thing, I always felt like I didn't love writing in school because there was someone telling me to do it. My big thing was I needed to be in control. I hated someone telling me what to do. . . . Now I keep a journal, but now it's like, I used to have a book and all I did was write. It was my book. Now, I draw. I sketch and write about my art."

With Anthony and his TeenStreet colleagues as guides, I began early in my second year to redefine the roles writing can take in a person's life. I also began to redefine how best to teach writing, particularly to students who have not experienced success or enjoyment in more traditional writing environments. Anthony speaks of writing as something he does when he wants to. Even as he says this, however, I get the impression from the way he looks at me and the tone of his voice that he wants me to understand how he feels, as if he is trying to tell me it's okay not to want to write, but it's not okay to think it is something you cannot learn or do.

Looking Back

Fifteen months earlier, it was the first rehearsal of a new ensemble. I arrived a half-hour early. I wanted to be in the room first, when it was empty, to take it all in and describe it as if I were describing the inside of an eggshell, cleansed of the distracting and messy elements of life.

After reintroducing myself to Ron, I hurried up the stairs, nearly running into a teenager. I pulled my notebook out of my backpack. Looking up, I saw a teenager onstage, jumping across the floor and kicking his legs and throwing his arms around like Bruce Lee. He stopped near the wall, frozen for a few seconds, saw me, nodded, and continued, moving back across the stage. He twisted in the air so forcefully that I felt the swirl of air 15 feet away.

He was a tall, lanky male whose tightly curled hair was styled in a box cut, the flat two-inch front extending straight up from his forehead, accentuating his narrow face. Whenever his movement brought him around to face me, he nodded and spun away. His eyes suggested amusement, and I did not know if it was with himself or me. Back across the stage he went, three or four more times, before finally stopping near a window. He leaned his elbows on the windowsill, letting his breathing ease a bit, and then turned toward me. His performance was something you would expect from kids on the playground, unaware of others watching. Caught by unintended eyes, they would beg off, giggle, and go on playing, now conscious of being observed. Yet this teenager, meeting my gaze throughout his performance and now in front of me, appeared sure of himself. I stood and introduced myself. He said his name was Ty. We shook hands. When I pulled my hand from his, his remained in the air.

I asked Ty if he was part of the ensemble, and he nodded.

"I'm interested in what the ensemble does and how it is different from school," I said.

Ty looked around as if I had awakened him to where he was. "I've been here forever," he said. He held his hands in front of him, the palms open and fingers spread, moving them with an orchestra conductor's rhythm. "This is my third year in this part of TeenStreet, but I was here before that. I know a lot about it. If there's anything you want to know, I can probably tell you."

Ty lived in the Cabrini Green public housing highrises a mile east of the field house. Early on in school he, like Anthony, was labeled with various learning disorders, among them attention deficit disorder. When I met him he was a part-time student at Columbia College, an arts-based school in downtown Chicago. Ty was not exaggerating much when he said he had been at TeenStreet forever. His mother was one of Free Street's instructors, and Ty had been coming to the third-floor studio since he was nine.

Ty, like Anthony, was a self-proclaimed rapper, offering that first rehearsal to rap for anyone who was interested but noting that his were always positive. "None of that negative stuff," he said, his hands moving back and forth.

The fingers and palms that worked the air so rhythmically when he spoke, hit the drums with a pulsating speed one moment and an easy backbeat the next. Ty carried in his head the different rhythms and beats he had heard or made up. On more than two occasions, as the script that coincided with my first year as a participant-observer was coming together in March and April, Ron asked Ty if he remembered a beat from jam sessions that had taken place in November and December. Ty nodded and banged it out for Ron to hear. "That's it," Ron said.

Of "Miss-Speakers" and Naming Our Experiences

Now, fifteen months later, here on the floor, I open my eyes a little bit, letting the whiteness of the light dissolve into the colors and shapes around me before opening them all the way. Anthony's breath softens. My thoughts move back and forth between him and Ty. Ty is not part of this year's ensemble, having completed his third production a few months earlier and now, at twenty-two, too old. The maximum age limit of the group is now twenty, a rule created at the beginning of this year's ensemble. Ty has dropped out of Columbia College, and I have not seen him in four months. He struggled through basic writing courses for two years before giving up. Later, when I do see him, he says he is looking for a job and hopes to go back to school soon. I find it hard to reconcile what I know about Ty with his educational experiences outside TeenStreet. Everything he did at TeenStreet belied the experiences he had in school, the former showing him to be not only an exceptional artist but also a dedicated and compassionate mentor; the latter, a "fish out of water," as another person once described Ty to me after spending a day with him at Columbia.

Ty recognized this dichotomy in his life, one of doing well at TeenStreet but not in school, one of being a strong and supportive presence for other TeenStreet teenagers but feeling out of place in other contexts. Recognizing this, he wrote a lot about how he felt. During a writing exercise midway through my first year, when asked to describe a character he would like to create, Ty wrote: "A miss-speaker: someone who hopes that people will think the way he does, do what he does—however he is powerless; he has been made powerless by those who have used and abused him. I feel like a miss-speaker myself." I think, outside of TeenStreet, that Ty felt that people missed or ignored what he had to say and, in effect, denigrated his experience.

Ty often wrote about his life and how others perceive him. Garrett Duncan (1996) suggests that such naming, or "giving critical clarity to one's location within the world," is critical to African Americans and other people of color in order to define their lives and who they are. Of his own life, Ty wrote:

Scary songs playing in my head like a broken record—
find a happy thought, they take it and wreck it.
Even in my home I don't feel safe because I feel an
evil image staring me in the face.
I'm telling you—it's a goddamn shame—evilghosts playing with my
mind like it's a game!
22 years old—will I live to see 23?
I don't know; this crazy shit keeps haunting me!
Call me crazy, but I keep having scary thoughts;
A gangster calls to me and suddenly I'm caught!
I can't walk the streets freely at night not knowing
about the prowling gangbangers in sight!
It doesn't matter if you're old or young;
I tell you—being afraid is no fun!
But tell me this—what ya gonna do
when shit like this comes haunting you?

The same perceptiveness that is demonstrated in Ty's words here was demonstrated in his performance at the first rehearsal. It is marked by being able to name what he experiences, to hone in on his own life and present it to others. Everything TeenStreet does has the aim of getting teenagers to be perceptive observers of their and others' lives, if only because the performances they create are based on those experiences. The characters Ty created, for example, reflected his life. He appeared aware of what his world looked like to others and negotiated his place in it, looking at all the angles and perspectives others might have of him:

Should I feel discriminated against because I
am black?
am poor?
have a behavioral disorder?
am the only 22 year old who likes the Power Rangers?
am afraid of the dark?
am afraid of being alone at night?
do not fit in?
am not famous?
don't value myself highly?
used to date white girls?
have approval from teachers that other students don't?
am the only black student in the class?
am different altogether?

As Ty's writing suggests, most of the writing done at TeenStreet is not only experiential but also reflective and analytical. The writing allows the teenagers to explore their lives through different perspectives. Much of the writing arises out of the movement and improvisational activities, and then is presented to the others for their interpretations, done through writing, improvisation, movement, and discussion. It moves, however, beyond journal-like expressions to communicating these expressions of self to others and seeing how others react. The interaction is reciprocal and often dialogical, as the teenagers' expressions are broadened in the interaction of words and actions, of writing and drama.

This Space Then and Now

Ron tells us to pull our left knees to our chests and hug them. Everyone's eyes are closed. Anthony's softened breathing becomes audible again with the start of warm-ups.

"Let your knee fall outward and move your leg in the socket," Ron says.

I put my hand on my knee and begin moving it in a figure-eight motion, feeling the muscles in my thighs and hamstrings loosen.

The dark green walls on both sides of me change to white about seven feet above the floor, where they angle inward, following the contours of the roof to form a cathedral ceiling with six large light fixtures hanging about three feet from the ceiling. Although about half of the windowpanes are covered with colored paper, black, green, and red, there is no need for the lights today. Sunlight shines through the dingy, uncovered panes, making visible the tiny dust particles that hang suspended like miniature orbs in the air above everybody. The teenagers who arrive first lay on the floor in the places caught in sunlight.

Eight feet above me, a black steel I-beam stretches across the stage, parallel with the back wall. Stage lights, some covered with red glass, some blue, some clear, hang, pointing in different directions, from the beam and three poles that run perpendicular with it to the wall above the door and windows. Opposite the windows, a riser holds about 40 opened folding chairs and three long benches shaped from 2×4's and plywood. Dumped on the chairs and benches are coats, musical instruments, clothes, shoes, book bags, and my tape recorder. Styrofoam cups, a liter of soda, a gallon of orange juice, and a bunch of bananas sit on an overturned wooden box. Pens are piled like fuel for a fire near the base of the platform, just off the stage floor. Next to them, scattered under a chair where they had been piled tall before sliding apart, are writing notebooks, one for each teen. Another hour will pass before they are used.

We switch to the right knee.

4:00 P.M., THURSDAY, OCTOBER 19, YEAR ONE

My first day at TeenStreet I sat in a chair in the middle of the riser and watched. The only teenager I had met, Ty, sat in a circle on the stage floor with eleven other teenagers and Ron. On the second page of my field notes, after over a page of room description, I quoted Ron as he finished speaking: "The performance is about us. . . . You have to have faith, faith in yourself and each other. . . . It ain't on your shoulders. We're all in this together. Go along for the trip, do your best, and try to get your judgmental thoughts out of your head."

Ron told the teenagers that over the next couple of months they would learn different warm-up exercises. The exercises would include improvisation. "The way that you develop being an actor and performer," he said, "is to explore things that are different from you. Try not to edit yourself or your negative voices."

Ron told them to begin to move slowly. "Put yourself on a beach, and waves are coming from all over. Every wave that hits you reverberates through your body. Start with small waves. What would that be like? How would that feel? The wave is easy, just lapping up against you as if you're on the beach. You feel it pushing up under you. Don't fight it, just relax."

While speaking, Ron let the waves wash over him. He rolled slowly back and forth. At first his movement was barely noticeable, but gradually he became more expressive. "As the wave gets stronger," he said, his voice in rhythm with his own movement, "it moves your whole body, pushing and pulling different parts of you in different directions and then the same direction." After a while, the waves pushed Ron to his knees and then back down again. He spoke of the waves getting stronger, telling the teenagers to imagine the possibilities of movement with a stronger wave, to imagine the wave's effect on their bodies as it begins to pick them up and move them. Some of the more experienced members, like Ty and Nancy, followed, rising to their feet and settling back onto the floor, rolling into others and bouncing back, eyes closed. The newest members rocked back and forth slowly. They opened their eyes and watched the others, their own movement stopping as they looked around. As Ron and the experienced teenagers let the waves toss them around the room, onto their feet and back to the floor, the new teenagers stayed in one place, standing and falling in unison.

"Don't stop," Ron exhorted Mona, who was standing still and watching everyone else. "Close your eyes and don't worry how you look. If you come in contact with someone, go with it."

The teenagers continued for another five minutes, in what would be their shortest movement exercise of the year. After they finished, Ron introduced them to Bryn. Bryn said he wanted to read a story he had written. "As I read," he said, "think about your secret life, about that inside you that is a secret you're just discovering." Before Bryn began, Ron told them to listen and try not to be judgmental. "Just take the story in," he said. "You'll hear so much more that way." The exercises; the admonitions to be nonjudgmental, to listen, and to interact; and the talk about the lives we can discover inside us, those secret lives, introduced themes that would take shape and grow with each successive rehearsal.

11:00 A.M., SATURDAY, OCTOBER 21, YEAR ONE

I participated only once in the movement exercises that first year. It was the first Saturday rehearsal. After talking to some of the teenagers before re-hearsal, without much thought, I left my notebook on a chair and joined every-one on the floor for warm-ups and the wave exercise. Afterward, Ron said to find a partner because he was going to introduce us to a couple of contact improvisation exercises that required working with someone else.

"Okay, you all take showers, right?" he said.

Everyone nodded, and a few people snickered.

"Yeah, well, one of you is going to act like you're the water and you got to be in contact with your partner at all times," Ron said. He put his hand on Elena's shoulder. "Feel that?" he asked.

She smiled and said yes. Although Elena was a newcomer to the ensem-ble, she had participated in summer workshops and dance classes at the field house and had seen past performances.

"Okay, if I push against you, you can do one of two things," Ron said. He gently pushed Elena, keeping a hand on her shoulder as she moved. Elena's legs stiffened, but she stood her ground.

When no one said anything, Ron asked, "Come on, what can you do?" Still no one answered. He pushed Elena harder, again without taking his hand away when he finished. Elena stepped sideways but quickly stepped back to where she had been. "What did you do?" Ron asked.

"Moved," Elena said.

"Right," Ron said. "Hear that?" He looked around and playfully pushed Elena again. "Pressure makes her move. When someone pushes against you, you can either move or what?"

Elena shrugged, and everyone looked at each other. "Or what?" said Ron again.

"Push back," Ty said. Elena nodded at Ty and smiled, leaning her shoul-der into Ron's outstretched hand.

"Right. You either push back or pull away," Ron said. "Now what you need to do is stay in contact with your partner. Keep connected as you roll your hand over people like it's water. Use both hands." He looked at Elena and said, "Let's try it. Start moving like in the wave exercise."

Elena began moving, circling around the room, dipping her shoulders and bending her legs and leaning sideways as she went. Ron followed at first, jumping alongside her and then behind her, one hand always on her body. He circled around her, bending as she bent and reaching up to the top of her head. The rest of us watched. After 30 seconds, they stopped.

Everyone stood silently. Some rocked back and forth on their feet. Elena took a deep breath as sweat glistened on her forehead and cheeks. Ron was dry, his pale skin beginning to redden.

Ron said, "Now, you can take this as sexual." He looked from face to face. "I mean, you'll be touching each other and, yeah, it looks sexual, but everything can be taken as sexual if you wanted to do that. Or you can see this as a way of connecting with others and letting go of some of your own inhibitions. If you see it as sexual, you're going to inhibit yourself and everyone will see that and you'll look like you're scared to death. Trust yourself and keep connected to your partner." He looked around. "Those of you who are water got to keep their hands on their partner. Like this." Ron stepped toward Elena and ran his hand across her back, shoulders, and neck.

Elena kept her mouth tightly closed. She rolled her eyes toward the ceiling and pulled away from Ron. He went with her. Whenever she pulled away from the reach of one hand, he reached with the other hand, never losing contact. When she pushed toward him, Ron changed hands just as it appeared she would push past him.

"When you're in the shower, the water goes everywhere, right?" Ron said, as he followed Elena around the circle again, slower this time but still jumping in front of her and appearing to lead for a moment. "Well, this is the same thing. When you're in the shower you move all about, right, but the water is still there, right?" He ran his hand down her side and onto her foot. Elena stopped. Ron stood up. "Use your judgment, people."

"You people who are taking showers need to do one of two things," Ron said.

"Push or pull," a couple of voices responded.

"Right. You either push against the pressure or pull away from the pressure," Ron said. "The water person must keep in contact and keep moving."

I teamed up with Elena, and Ron stepped off to the side. We all started, and someone laughed. Ron said to stop, and everyone turned toward him. He walked to the middle of the room. "There's no reason for anyone to be laughing. I mean, this ain't that funny, at least not in that way."

We started again, and for the next four minutes we moved across the stage, one person's hand moving across another's body, first the arm, then the chest, shoulder, neck, face, down the leg to the foot and back up. Feet and legs rose in the air. People rolled across the floor, bending and ducking along the way. "Don't try to get away from your partner," Ron yelled. "It's easy to do, but that's not the purpose here." We switched roles and began again.

When we finished, everyone was out of breath. A couple of teenagers pulled off their sweat tops while others pushed their hair out of their eyes. Sweat beaded across foreheads and hairlines. Ron introduced us to another contact improvisation exercise. One partner acted as a contact zone while the other quickly moved about touching her. The one being touched had to respond as if he were being pushed, doing so in an exaggerated or slow-motion fashion. The one doing the touching looked as if she were dabbing paint on a moving person.

Half of us watched from the side of the stage as the other half did the movement. After a few minutes, we switched places. When we finished, we talked about the movement and watching others. Ty said watching others reminded him of stories.

Nancy agreed. "Just watching, you make conclusions about what others are doing and why. You interpret what you see." Other teenagers nodded in agreement.

"Yeah, but what about those who are doing it?" Ron said.

Donna said she wasn't thinking when she was out there. She couldn't think because if she did, she would start acting unnatural.

"What's that mean?" someone asked.

"It means I just had to move and not think about it," she said.

"How did you feel when you were out there?" Ron asked Mona.

"It gave me a headache," she said. "All that moving, my head started hurting."

"Okay," Ron said, and laughed. "If that continues as you get used to doing this, then we have a problem."

"You have to be playful to do this," Ty added, holding up his hands. "You have to just let go and play around with your partner like you're trying to keep him moving, trying to be unpredictable but not elusive."

"You couldn't think about it, though," someone said.

"Do you think the watchers see things the same way as those who are doing the movement?" Ron asked.

"No way," Ty said. "I wasn't thinking of stories when I was out there. I was too busy just moving." Others nodded in agreement. "Yeah, when you're doing the moving, you're not thinking about what is next, you're watching your partner and just responding."

Ron nodded his head and said, "Yeah, well, that's it, I guess. You give yourself up to your partner."

Ty's comment about stories stuck with me. I wrote it down, as well as what it felt like when I was out there and then what it was like to watch the others. Watching did make me think of stories I had heard. I tried to make connections with my own experiences.

Later on, Ron tried to draw on teenagers' experiences to get them to act out certain feelings, to bring forth those feelings from inside as a way to initiate and fuel the movement, which I suppose is a way of bringing stories to bear on the doing. This, however, was only the second rehearsal. He wanted them to experience moving and interacting with someone else, with no language mediating the movement and interaction. Communication came through the touching and watching of one's partner.

I didn't participate in any other movement exercises that first year, because I wasn't asked and didn't think it was part of my researcher role at the time. I focused on the notion of stories, on the movement being interpreted as stories. I forgot about the act of moving and what that meant to the performer.

12:30 P.M., SATURDAY, JANUARY 11, YEAR TWO

We are an hour and a half into rehearsal. Fifteen minutes earlier we finished a movement exercise that evolved from the warm-ups. During the exercise, later named Watusi, the teenagers worked on characters they wanted to play in the performance, allowing the characters to interact with one another to see how they responded. It began with everyone in a circle—a whole-group exercise where everyone did the same thing, responded to others. Using peripheral vision, the teenagers followed others' movements, never initiating any movement of their own. The exercise started with the slightest twinge being picked up by someone else. With each response, the twinge grew and, of course, with each growth of movement more imitations grew until everyone was moving in response to everyone else, trying to imitate others while others imitated them. The only rule was to follow, not lead.

As the exercise developed, Ron gave directions to people. He told Denise to dance in the middle of the group. No one was to follow her, however. He told Chau, Terri, Sharon, Yusuf, and Tonya to add voice or start talking or singing to themselves or others. He told Nick to begin a stream-of-consciousness spiel about how he felt.

"Rocker, maniac, maniac," he began, "I'm a maniac, not Mexican, Italian, a maniac . . . " Donna imitated Nick, reflecting his words to show she was upset with him. Ron yelled over the noise for everyone to use peripheral vision, to pay attention to what was going on around them. "Karen, follow Elena," he said. "Anthony, follow Chau." After ten minutes, Ron told everyone but Denise to find an ending. Denise continued to dance.

As the teenagers caught their breath, Ron talked about becoming possessed by a character. He said: "When you get to the point where you think you are the character, when you become possessed by a character, then take that character and begin having a conversation, embody it." He told them to take a few moments and stand still—"still like a frog with the energy of your emotions ready to explode—and find your character again." After a minute, they started the next movement with eyes closed. They began by using geo-metric shapes as they moved, walking in squares, circles, ovals, and triangles, and weaving them together and letting them grow, shrink, and evolve into other shapes.

For five minutes, Ron talked as they moved, saying: "Respond to how you feel, what's going on inside you. Begin to travel, to use space and find out what's going on. When you're ready, slowly begin to open your eyes until you see shadows. Then heighten what's cookin' inside you. Add a little sound. Heighten and extend your movement." He said to begin interacting with other characters. The room was abuzz with voices.

Charles grabbed his bass and set up in the corner, hitting the low notes so hard that the sound echoed across the room. Underneath all the noise, Tonya sang a Christian Sunday School song: "This little light of mine, I'm going to let it shine. Let it shine, let it shine wherever I go. I'm going to let it shine wherever I go. I'm going to let it shine." Yusuf stood in the middle of the stage and rapped under his breath. When Tonya walked over to where Charles was playing, Ron yelled, "Good, good, you can't do anything wrong here, just go with it."

While I was writing, Bryn walked in and sat down. Ron smiled at him. After five minutes, Ron told the group to find an ending. Afterward, they took a short break.

When they came back together, Bryn had them write about the move-ment and their characters. He told them they could write from the character's perspectives or about how they felt during the movement. After fifteen min-utes, they read to themselves what they wrote. "Now write about your charac-ter in ecstasy," Bryn said. "What is ecstasy for your character? What does that character want more than anything?"

Later, the ensemble will break into groups of dancers, musicians, and improvisation actors, and Bryn will call individual teenagers down to the stu-dio lobby to read what they wrote, discuss imagery and meaning, and talk about revision and others' writing ideas.

Now, however, as they write, I walk over to the windows. Leaning on a sill, I press my cheek against the cold glass. The sun glint on the windows across the street makes them appear impenetrable, like steel covers over the glass. Reflected back to me is the field house and me. As I listen to the others write, I remember a writing exercise from the first month of last year's ensemble.

It was only the fourth rehearsal. Bryn had finished describing an elaborate writing exercise for the second time. It included looking out the window and describing what one saw. Along with that, the teenagers wrote about what they saw in the room as a movement exercise was going on and what they looked like as they looked in a mirror. They moved from writing area to writing area—the window, a mirror off to the side of the stage, and a chair next to the stage—three or four at a time as the others did the movement exercise. Bryn prepared them for the exercise by speaking about the subtle differences of perception people have even when they are looking at the same thing.

The second year's ensemble did something similar a few weeks earlier, but it was the exercise that first year that I remembered. Someone, I don't remember who, wrote: "I could see an old man in the window. He was next to the radiator. He was covered in a sheet. The sheet had 3 rips in it."

Later, Ty took these lines and built on them until they became the following in *MadJoy*:

I could see in the window. The old men were next to the radiator.
One was covered in a sheet. The sheet had 3 rips in it.
Next to the radiator they sit, at war with themselves.
Everywhere actions in the brain. Action. Action.
Action.
Bullets penetrating signs, barriers.
A run-down store front.
Happy, but at war?
The tall buildings they lived in were like blocks of loneliness.
They are gray and pale, and the trucks that drive past . . .
. . . it is a beer truck, carrying "escape" in the back.

Their eyes find the Miller LIGHT sign flashing like a
weird hypnotic gesture.
Bzzzzzzzzzzzzzzzzzzzzzzzzzzzzzzzzzzzzzzzzzzzzzzzzzzzzz.

That day, however, after the lines about the old man, the radiator, and the sheet were written, Bryn took the paper and reread it aloud a couple of times. He ran the fingers of his free hand across his hair and adjusted his black-rimmed glasses. "Geez, what is it about this description?" he said.

"It's stark," said Ty. "It's almost like watching a movie, like you feel the camera moving in closer to the old man."

"Something personal is being revealed," someone said.

"It leaves a lot to be interpreted," another added, "like it involves you in the seeing."

Bryn asked what kind of language was used in the passage. He got comments about imagery and starkness of description.

"It makes you see it like it is," someone said. A couple of teenagers agreed.

"That's good," Bryn said, letting the discussion ease a bit. The group read the rest of the pieces and discussed them in similar fashion.

When the group was ready to stop for the day, Bryn asked if anyone else wanted to say something. Elena, who had been quiet for most of the writing session, said that she thought it interesting that someone wrote about the garbage outside and that there are probably rats everywhere. Se, indeed, had written in response to what she saw outside: "An alley with garbage outside of the garbage can. It really needs to be cleaned. I know there has to be a rat somewhere."

A couple of the teenagers giggled, and someone said, "Yeah, it's not very pretty."

Others had written similar sentences, such as, "I see the dilapidated building with lonely, cold windows and a sad, bare room, empty of life. It is hollow." Of the same building, I think, another teenager had written, "I am gazing outside at a great magnificent chimney. How beautiful."

"I live in this neighborhood," Elena said, smiling. "I see the garbage, too, but when I look out I see things from my childhood. I see the street corner and remember me and my friends standing there and talking."

Bryn nodded. He took a deep breath and smiled. Bryn, a playwright, had confessed to me the first day I observed TeenStreet that it was his first day as a writing instructor and he was nervous. Tall, with a deep voice and dark, curly hair, he commanded attention with his presence and voice, yet he understood the importance of listening and not making pronouncements about the teenagers' writing. He always responded positively and enthusiastically, prefacing his comments with phrases such as, "I really could see that" or "Wow." He took the time to discuss imagery and what he thought the writer was trying to convey. He always allowed the writer to respond. Often during such conversations, the meaning and imagery of what had been written were fleshed out and made fuller.

What Bryn did not say about the writing that day, but what I have come to realize is ingrained in every movement, improvisation, voice, and writing activity done at TeenStreet, is the importance of one's own and others' experiences and interpretations to one's understanding of the world. Students are learning to make sense of their worlds and to see how that sense affects others. Writing is part of that, as Elena demonstrated in her response to the written descriptions of her neighborhood. Elena already had images of the neighborhood outside the window that no amount of writing could dispel and that other teenagers' comments were not capturing. She lived here.

From my position by the window, face pressed against the glass, looking north, I see the top of the new elementary school built next to the old, and the expressway three blocks away, angling toward us, semis and cars flickering between buildings. The expressway slices through the neighborhood, forcing residential streets to end abruptly. It dips down to street level, speeding cars separated from kids playing in the streets by cement pylons and a chain-link fence. It is nearly quiet in the room. All I can hear are the scrape of pens across paper, the exhaling of breath through partly closed mouths.

3:15 P.M., SATURDAY, JANUARY 11, YEAR TWO

In a month, the writing, movement, voice, and improvisation workshops end, as production of the script begins to take up more rehearsal time. With the script in draft stages, the teenagers start rehearsing parts and revising, working on music, movement, and dance. Tony, a former ensemble member, starts coming every week to help with the choreography and teach dance steps. Bryn comes less often, and when he does it is to look at the script and make suggestions. Because I will not be a part of the production, my participation ends, and I am back on the platform observing.

Rehearsals usually end with Ron talking about the coming weeks, particularly the next rehearsal. We come together in a circle on the floor. Today is no different. Ron highlights things he thought went well and notes things needing improvement. He is quick and purposeful, staring at the floor in front of him or referring to notes he took during rehearsal. A couple of teenagers look at their watches, but most lean back on their elbows or against each other and listen.

Only four of the teenagers live in the neighborhood, so most will change clothes and catch a bus or train home. A couple of them drive or will be picked up. Most are from low-socioeconomic-strata homes, with some from the West Side, some from the South Side, and a couple from the North Side of Chicago. It's a mixed group: three Whites, three Latinos, five African Americans, and one Asian, with some going to private high schools, some to public schools, and a few having graduated.

Occasionally I drive some of the teenagers who live on the West Side home. It is usually Mona, however, who asks for a ride, nearly every Saturday, even when she is going to the Henry Horner Homes, a Near West Side public housing project, to baby-sit cousins. It's not out of my way, so I drive her there, too.

Mona is a petite African-American woman, quiet and reserved until pressed about her opinion of something. Then she looks at whomever she is speaking to and speaks emphatically. She is quick to talk about what she thinks is wrong with the world and defend herself when she feels she is not being treated with respect. Her writing shows the same philosophical forethought and self-determination.

Mona shows up to rehearsals in bright blue and yellow nylon sweats that are too big for her. They are part of her high school track uniform. During rehearsals she is often quiet. Invariably, however, she'll ask Bryn to clarify a writing exercise, wanting to know what she is supposed to write about, a refrain reminiscent of my own students when I was teaching. She listens, nods her head, and starts writing. When she reads what she wrote, she is matter-of-fact, her face bent toward the page that sits on her lap. Her words, however, pulsate with life, her descriptions more vivid than if what she describes were being played out on the wall, like a movie, before our eyes. For example, upon returning to the ensemble after giving birth to a baby girl, Mona wrote in early November of her and my second year:

Birth—the moment
life and death
PAIN
scream
crying
bending fingers
trouble
don't know what's next
creating
developing
lose, win, angry, mad at my boyfriend.

On our drives west—a straight shot across the city on Division Street through some of Chicago's poorest neighborhoods—Mona tells me how her week has gone. She does not know how much longer she can stay in Teen-Street. "I got too much to do," she says. This is the second of her two years at TeenStreet. Both years she quit in early spring, the first because she was pregnant and the second to take care of her baby and concentrate on school. The scripts for both years ring with her words.

We talk about the West Side. Mona's stories are different from mine, although we only live two blocks apart. She hates the West Side, recalling being robbed on the corner of Division and Pine as we drive past. She tells me about a friend of hers, "a neighbor boy," she says, only nineteen years old. She talks about watching him grow up as if she is older than him. She is seventeen. He was killed recently, and she says she cannot get it out of her mind. The killers took his body and buried it under a pile of leaves in his yard so that his momma found him. "Can you imagine that?" she says.

"No, I can't," I say.

When I tell Mona a few weeks later that I am moving to another Chicago neighborhood that spring, she says she hopes one day to do the same. Mona does not come back to rehearsal the next week, and Ron tells me she called to say she quit.

I have heard and read many stories about where the teenagers live, but seldom is place evoked. I know where they live because they tell me. With Mona, it's different because I know the neighborhood, too, having lived there for nine years.

The teenagers write and talk about their lives and the lives of people around them. As I move outward from TeenStreet, on foot or in my car, my experiences of a rehearsal or my memory of a conversation with a teenager are imbued with the landscape around me, and what I remember reading or hearing is made real—confirmed, maybe—by what I see, although I know it is impossible for me to know these teenagers' lives as they know them. Mona lived two blocks from me, but her stories are so different from mine. I have their stories to help me see, to broaden my understanding beyond what I could possibly experience on my own.

The teenagers' stories are shaped by different contexts. The one thing we have in common, however, is the context in which our stories are shared. In choosing to write about TeenStreet, I focus on that context, knowing it can never be separated from the many contexts the teenagers and I bring to it, knowing that the experiences we all bring to TeenStreet shape who we are and what we are to become together, even if only for a short time.

EVOLVING PERSPECTIVE

During my first year at TeenStreet I was confident about what I observed and what it meant. I understood my purpose as a literacy ethnographer to understand how literacy is constructed and used at TeenStreet. I was guided by the principle that literacy and human agency are so entwined that one without the other left both poverty-stricken. Human agency, as such, not only depends on language, with human experience contingent on language—that is, on how the agent defines experience using language—but, in many cases, on written language, too.

My association of literacy with agency was an ideology with little historical support and grounded in the logocentric views I described in Chapter 1. Such a view is prominent in what Harvey Graff (1979) calls the "literacy myth," with the myth at one time or another being that literacy rates correlate with things as varied as economic advancement, crime rates, fertility rates, and cognitive abilities. The principles underlying this ideology guided my first year at TeenStreet.

Based on my field notes from that first year, I did not fully consider the experience represented in the movement, improvisation, or even writing exercises. I honed in on the writing and what these other activities might contribute to writing development and saw the interpretation of individuals' stories as primary to what was happening at TeenStreet. I seldom considered the importance of the process of writing one's stories, which includes these other exercises, much less the importance of living and performing them. It was as if the product of writing was what mattered and not how the writer got there.

Once I became a participant in the second year, I continued to see the significance of language use, both written and oral, to the other exercises. In addition, however, I started to see the experiential nature of the somatic and mental imagery as preceding language use and, thus, writing, and as grounding language in the prosaic in an effort to help teenagers reclaim or re-create language that speaks to their lives as they live them and not as they are perceived by others.

The guidelines for my observations shifted after my first year: I maintained that we must know from where it is we stand in time and space—we must contemplate our own perspective and experience of the world—to know and interact with others. Yet we must also honor in others that which we claim for ourselves, that same uniqueness of place and time. From our own time and space, others help us know the self even more. It is an ever-evolving and dialogical process where we are constantly looking inward and outward.

The guiding principle of my research evolved to where I realized that we are individual body and blood first and that others, too, are individuals, bodies and blood; that everything we do prepares us for using language and not vice versa, even as the two—language and experience—converge into reciprocity.

I observed the TeenStreet activities my first year from a chair, except for the second rehearsal. I did not plan to come back for a second year until a few weeks before the second ensemble began. I saw the final performance of *MadJoy* that fall and came away thinking that I had missed out on an opportunity that first year. To reformulate an old theater adage: The play was the thing. Not the play as in what was scripted and performed, but the play that got the teenagers to where they were, the actions and interactions during workshops and rehearsals, the playing out of experience that went into creating a script. I missed that.

When I asked Ron if I could come back, I said I wanted to participate in some of the activities. He smiled and said he wondered when I was going to get involved. I had, however, begun secretly participating in the writing exercises the first month of the first year I was a participant-observer. I wrote as the teenagers wrote, using the same prompts and reflecting on the activities I observed in ways suggested by Bryn.

That first year I also reflected on what the teenagers were doing as they participated in movement and improvisation exercises. I moved away from only describing what I saw to describing how what I saw made me feel and think and bringing my own life into the description. Thus, my initial forays into the movement, improvisation, and voice exercises came through literacy use, but such participation only whetted my appetite for experiencing what the teenagers were experiencing.

As I watched the teenagers warm up during a November rehearsal that first year, I wrote about how cold it was outside. We had gotten six inches of snow the night before, and I had shoveled the sidewalks around my house before I came to rehearsal. Physically, I still felt a chill in my bones, and the warmth on my skin that comes from exerting oneself on a cold winter's day. I watched Jim and Bonnie as they lay side by side on the floor, Jim in front of Bonnie, five feet between them. Their arms and legs moved in unison in a sweeping motion across the floor. They raised and lowered their heads and feet together and twisted their bodies in the same direction. They moved slowly, trying to trick the other or catch the other being less perceptive. Their movements, however, were concentrical, as if their bodies were hanging from a pendulum, with each part—their hands, arms, torso, legs, and feet—at the end of smaller pendulums. I watched them and, in a flurry, wrote:

In the morning there were six inches of snow
On the ground, soft as a newly frosted cake
In a baker's window.
We found a spot in the front yard and made
crescent moons,
Our backs bent as we lay on our sides,
Arms stretched,
So that our stomachs got wet.
For a moment we were two moons. Then our feet
trailed away,
moon dust, toward the porch,
A fire on my cheeks.

That first year, I continued to reflect in similar ways on what the teenagers were doing. I literally was following Ty's lead from that second rehearsal: I saw stories in what I observed. By the end of that first year, I was confident about what I knew about TeenStreet writing, but I didn't know enough about the creative process and the nature of possibilities and exploration that arise through perspective-taking and the use of imaginal interaction, that is, the interaction both of perspectives and of activities. I did not understand how possibilities are shaped and ever-growing in the interactions that are the Teen-Street creative process. I viewed TeenStreet as a text—a site—to be read and understood and, later, re-authored.

With an opportunity to return and participate, TeenStreet became not a text but an event, open to possibilities. It is an event holding out possibilities for myself and others, which is what makes TeenStreet successful, I think. When I saw only as an observer I missed what Slavic language scholar Gary Morson (1996) calls the sideshadows of an event, or the multiple possibilities that all events hold even as only one possibility is played out. I missed what anthropologist Victor Turner (1986) termed the luminality of ritual, a movement of real transcendence that, when it is over, leaves one's life changed.

I began experiencing these possibilities in the writing I did. I pulled from my own experience and found those stories of which Ty spoke. Yet full participation, particularly if one is to reclaim language and use it in naming one's own existence, requires perspective-taking beyond the scope of language, and this is what TeenStreet offers teenagers. Participation carries with it more than opportunities for literacy development; participation offers other mediational tools, such as mental and somatic signs and gestural and musical expression, that augment language use and voice development. Participation also brings with it responsibility, responsibility that rings with M. M. Bakhtin's (1993) notion that there is no alibi in existence, that we are responsible for responding to others from our own place and time. We are responsible for honing our own voices.

3

The Joinery: Human Interaction and the Telling of Stories

An ensemble production hinges on one's awareness of time and place—embodied as presence on stage—in relation to others on stage and in the audience. Ron, Anita, and Bryn saw this awareness and interaction as a way of expression that, although unique to each teenager, allows each to draw on others' experiences to create possible ways of acting in their own lives. These possibilities, like Morson's sideshadows, are agentive ways of defining and addressing the world, meaning that they are ways for teenagers to name their worlds and posit ways of acting or living that are particular to themselves and their communities. One experience in particular shows how perspective-taking and interacting played themselves out in discussion and practice at TeenStreet.

We were six weeks into rehearsals during my second year when Ron invited Mars Williams, a well-known Chicago saxophonist, to sit in on some improvisational jam sessions with the teenagers. Ron asked him to talk about his music and creative process.

Mars arrived during warm-ups. When we finished, he asked if we wanted to jam. We pulled chairs onto the stage and grabbed instruments. Donna started it off on the bongo drums and everyone fell in, with Mars's saxophone adding a new sound. Tonya came in on the drum and everything that came afterward followed her rhythm. Midway through, some of the teenagers traded instruments. Ten minutes later, people began pulling out. The sound was like a comet, heavy and massive in front, with a lazy, spiraling tail that breaks apart and hangs in midair at the end. The drums and sax pulled everyone along. Mona, Anthony, and Sharon hit the floor and chair legs with drum sticks. Ron, Yusuf, and Tonya banged on the drums. Terri and Denise clapped out the rhythm with their hands. Mars sat his saxophone down and leaned forward as the others played. He smiled and rocked back and forth. Ron raised his hands, signaling to bring the sound down and find an ending.

Later, Mars played a track from a Thelonius Monk CD and told us to listen for the anticipation of each note, particularly the space between notes— that stillness—that creates tension in the listening. "We can't wait for that note," he said. "The stillness makes us want it bad, and when it comes it can floor us."

Afterward, Ron asked Mars about the stillness in his own music.

Mars said stillness is a time for him to rest and listen to others play. "I'm leaving space for others, but more than that, I'm waiting for my moment to come in even when I don't know when that happens."

"You got to let the stillness come to you," Ron said, "not force it."

Mars nodded and put on a Sun Ra CD. He asked the teenagers to think about what goes through their minds when they listen to it.

When the track was over, Mars said he listens to others' music to find his own place in it, as if he were part of the recording. He is deciding what role to take or how to respond. "In music, I can take the melodic or rhythmic role."

Ron asked him to show us. Mars picked up his sax and played. When he finished, Ron said the melodic approach is like talking.

"Actually, you could replace any note with words," Mars said.

Yusuf asked if word jazz would be melody with words.

"Sure," Mars said. "You can have sound under words." He clicked on Sun Ra again and, using his saxophone, showed how improvisation is listening to what's around you and complimenting or negating it. He jumped in at various places in the music, transforming the Sun Ra piece into something else than what was on the CD.

When he finished, Mars asked if we wanted to try it. He started off on his saxophone, stopped, and told everyone to look for ways to respond to others, to not be afraid to pull out and listen and then jump back in. He started again, and one by one everyone followed. The sound was looser than before, moving in different directions only to be pulled back by others. There were moments when the drums fell away and the voices of Tonya and Sharon overrode everything else. Charles picked up his bass and pulled the entire group along in a thumping rhythm that was complimented by short blasts from Mars's saxophone and quick, pulsating interludes on the drums. We brought it to an end in an explosion of sounds.

"I liked that," Mars said as he sat his saxophone down. "I could feel the interacting."

"It felt like we were playing off each other," Yusuf said.

"Yeah, it was much more unpredictable, too," Mars said.

"Do you think about where you're going to fit in as you play it?" Ron asked.

"Definitely," Mars said. "I'm thinking about it. Anticipating. I look for the tension to take me somewhere."

"Do you ever miss your moment?" Ron asked.

"Yeah."

Everyone laughed. "It happens to us, too," Ron said. "What do you do?"

"I initiate a new improv."

"The act of missing creates a new thing," Ron said.

"That's part of it," Mars said. "Improv should be spontaneity. You do have certain things to work on, though."

"Boundaries?" Ron said.

"Yes."

"It's the same with our movement," Ron said. "You ever have anything with no structure?"

"Sure," Mars said.

"What happens when someone throws a bomb in it?" Ron asked.

Mars shrugged his shoulders. "Try to create a cohesiveness. You need to listen and pick your approach. Work with or against."

"Against it is still support?" Ron asked.

Mars smiled. "I think so. You're still creating something together. In a group, you think of your role. It doesn't need to be spelled out. You choose your role, but you still need to define it. Take your chances and make that part of your role. Sometimes it doesn't work. You just try and learn from your mistakes."

Ron will repeat this refrain in coming weeks: Create or find your place within established frameworks, but don't be afraid of pushing at the boundaries of that framework. He tells the teenagers to be creative yet responsive.

MULTIPLE POSSIBILITIES IN THE WRITING OF ETHNOGRAPHIES

In this chapter, I speak of the power of experience, real and imagined, and of story, fiction and nonfiction, in shaping one's consciousness and perspective of the world. Later chapters use these descriptions and interpretations to define experience's capacity to nurture and enhance consciousness and perspective-taking and, in turn, literacy. This chapter establishes the limitations and necessity of all human perspective-taking. I want to take one strand and, beginning with my experience and understanding of TeenStreet and the teenagers' places within that understanding, weave together what I understand of storying and how it illuminates possible existences while never fully giving away all possibilities.

In considering how to describe TeenStreet and convey the teenagers' and my own experiences, and to speak to issues of literacy that transcend the TeenStreet context, I am compelled to push at the boundaries of traditional research reportage. I am reminded of Ellison's invisible man (1947/1990) when he realized that he was invisible and why: "It goes a long way back, some twenty years. All my life I had been looking for something, and everywhere I turned someone tried to tell me what it was" (p. 15). The defining of that something for oneself is as significant to one's understanding as is the looking. The invisible man lived life based on how others thought he should live, first on what others, in a segregated society, expected of a young African-American man of talent and then what others expected of the post-World War II Socialist man. Understanding who he was began when he realized that he was no one but himself, and for that only he was accountable. Although what he had learned from others was important, it was through his own experiences in relation to what others had said and done that he created his own identity. In going underground, the invisible man did not so much reject what he had learned from others as reformulate it in relation to his own experiences. The invisible man literally had to go underground, away from others, to learn this about himself.

It was among others, however, with conscious reflection on his own perspective in relation to others', that the invisible man developed his identity. In the sewers of New York, the invisible man consciously defined himself because he was left to contemplate his being and not live in relationship with others. His self-identity reached an endpoint, defined by what had happened with no consideration of or influence from what is happening while underground. Unlike characters in fiction, however, we seldom can go underground literally or figuratively. We must define ourselves within the contexts in which we exist, based largely on our interpretation and reflection on our interactions with others. TeenStreet strives to make this process of defining ourselves a conscious activity.

SEEING POSSIBILITIES IN EVERYDAY LIFE

The present ethnography is not so much about literacy per se as it is about affording students opportunities to express themselves, with writing being one means of doing this. Writing can help people become aware of expanding possibilities but is not an end in itself. Possibilities can be as narrow as believing there are choices to be made in life or as broad as living life as dynamically as one desires, knowing that the road ahead branches out in ever-growing and ever-converging directions. Knowing there are multiple possibilities arises from ever-expanding experiences, both real and vicarious, and from human interaction. In believing one has possibilities and in pursuing them, one becomes an agent in the world. It is knowing that what *has* happened is not necessarily what had to happen, or that what is going to happen is never preordained.

Yet a story, with a beginning, middle, and end, can close down life even if its theme may be to show life as open and full of possibilities. Gary Morson (1996) suggests that there are ways to reflect the openness and possibilities of life in stories. Stories can allow for sideshadowing, with both characters and readers recognizing that events are filled with multiple possibilities that could have happened even if they did not. The writing of this book is an act of imaginal interaction, the weaving of multiple stories that, by definition, is the TeenStreet creative process.

To demonstrate this process, I offer the following story from my own life and its evolution as a significant experience fraught with possibilities that took time to be revealed. It is a story that, although based on my childhood experience, took shape within the TeenStreet context among other stories and activities and came to mean something else to me in that process. Over time, I came to see my own work as a participant-observer begin to represent what Ron, Anita, and Bryn were trying to get the teenagers to do. Ethnography can offer a meta-awareness of existence. It is a consciously focused look at life, one similar to the conscious perspective-taking and interaction Ron describes.

I found much in my observations that spoke to who I am and how I perceive the world. The story that follows is about my perceptions of my relationship with my mother. I spent the majority of my youth separated from my mother. A memory I had of her during our separation was of her trying to paint the outside of our house and never finishing, so that two years later, after she had left my father and me, I was moving empty paint cans and hardened paintbrushes out of the garage at my father's behest, literally removing the last remnants of her. I do not think my father had me do this for that reason. Most likely, he wanted the garage cleaned.

The ground around the back of the house was littered with paint chips and wood splinters. The siding was speckled white, bare of paint and mildewed in many places where it had been readied for paint but never painted. Yet such connections—cleaning garages and forgetting someone else's existence, seeing paint chips and ruminating on memories of others—are not necessarily the stuff of ten-year-olds' consciousness, or even adults' for that matter. Such connections require ruminating on one's life and others', and in ruminating, one's memory and life are changed.

Before my father—really my stepfather—there was only my mom and I, a teenage woman and her son. What dominates my memory of our time together is her sitting at the kitchen table at night, making plans, thinking about how her life would be if she did this or that. She was a waitress. Late into many nights, I watched her from the far end of the hall, only the corner of the kitchen table visible, wafts of cigarette smoke disentangling in the air above her head, scratching out notes to herself with a pencil.

The next morning, the ashtray, coffee cup, and notes would still be on the table. The apartment would be quiet, the light shining through the windows a grayish hue that made everything soft and clean. My mother would be in bed, covers pulled up around her body, air still stale with the smell of cigarettes. What I thought about all this then I don't remember now.

I knew then that my real father had been killed when I was two. What it meant to my mom, however, I only recently learned. My aunt—my mother's sister—told me the story of his death nine years ago. When she told me, I had seen my mother only once in fifteen years. If stories are avenues to understanding, increasing possibilities for the traveler, then this one was like a newly constructed highway.

My real father's family owned a large construction company in northern Kentucky. I did not know this when I was a child, or anything else my aunt told me. My mother and father met when she was fifteen and he was nineteen. She was sixteen when I was born. His family did not want him to have anything to do with my mother or me.

My aunt said my mother was "stupidly in love with him." She quit school and tried to use me to win my father back. And it started to work, my aunt said. My father started coming around, and he and my mother went on a couple of dates. His family did not know.

My father had a friend whose father owned a butcher shop. His friend was learning the business. The place smelled of raw meat and blood, and the floor behind the counter was thick with animal fat. As my aunt told me this, I could see her thinking, trying to re-create that room. "It was like being in a skating rink, and when it got too bad the owner would drop a little sawdust on the floor around the saw and cutting block," she said. My father's friend did not like that because it stuck to his shoes.

On July 9, 1963, my father was in the shop joking around and slipped on the greasy floor, hitting his head on the corner of a cutting block. I have imagined what he must have been doing to fall like that. I see him possibly doing many different things, from acting like the floor was a skating rink to climbing on top of the cutting board and walking on the edge as if it were a tightrope. It is even possible, I have thought, that he was already dying when the accident happened, a tumor already on his brain.

He died three days later, and my mother nearly went crazy. "She was too young for that," my aunt said. "She just didn't know how to handle it, and I can remember me and your Aunt Pat holding her down, and your mom was a little girl still, no more than ninety pounds." I know my aunt says this to explain my mother's actions, but I am not sure what about her actions needs explaining.

To me, the story explains much of what I saw in my mother and could not account for. It is a story she never told me. Only observing her was not enough, and the story itself took a long time in coming. So what am I to make of my perspective of my mother during my childhood and my later understanding of this time? We can never be sure of what we do not know, or of what we see or are told. We can only keep pursuing more experiences, more stories, more voices.

THE CONVERGENCE OF ETHNOGRAPHY AND LIFE

This story took shape as something I wanted to share during rehearsals at TeenStreet. I began playing with the idea of how to tell it during my first year at TeenStreet. During a rehearsal in December of my second year, I wanted to tell it again. David Schein, the executive director of Free Street, was leading the rehearsal because Ron was out of town. Everything we did that day, including the movement exercises, incorporated sound. A year earlier David had led a rehearsal, introducing the same voice exercises, which became part of later rehearsals. The same happened after this rehearsal as voice exercises came to take a more prominent role in rehearsals.

After an hour of movement exercises with voice, Bryn took over. He got us in a circle on the floor and read a passage about the writer's ear by Grace Paley. Paley wrote of having two ears, figuratively speaking, one that listens for structure and the other for poetry. Bryn related this idea to the Japanese Noh theater idea that story is "built out of your bones and in your language, but written so that others see it." Story, according to Noh theater, is the poetry of the body. Helping others understand requires providing a structure familiar to others. A writer digs within herself for what she knows, looking to excavate the story in ways familiar to others.

Bryn talked about looking for those times in one's life that are rich. These times are transforming moments, with one's life being changed. Rich moments are moments we can turn to later and mark as definitive of who we are. As Bryn spoke, I thought about my mother and the story my aunt told me. Knowing this story gave new meaning to my life. It had settled into my bones to become part of who I am, changing my memory of many past events. I realized that to tell it, I had to give it structure. Structure, however, means more than shaping words and sentences. It requires courage to expose oneself, to reveal the marrow of one's bones and find one's own words and not just buy "off the shelf."

Bryn gave an example of a rich experience from his own life. He recalled going to see a play when he was a teenager. Sitting there, he realized he wanted to be a playwright. He went home and started writing. Although it was hard, he continued to write and felt he could do it. The act of writing convinced Bryn of the rightness of it, but it was the moment he realized he wanted to be a playwright that transformed his life.

As Bryn finished, Yusuf leaned forward. He said, "I know that feeling. When I was young, my mom died. I was scared and didn't know what was going to happen to me or my brother." He hesitated a moment, as if trying to figure out what to say next.

Bryn said, "Yeah, we hold onto those minutes and they're clear in our minds—"

"Yeah," Yusuf said.

Charles said, "I remember the exact moment when I realized that I could accomplish anything if I tried. I came home from school and just felt like I was in control of my life even though I was still only a kid, and it's like I didn't worry about things as much after that."

It was quiet for a moment, and then Yusuf, staring at the floor in the middle of the circle we formed as a group, said, "I realized that my mom expected a lot from me before she died. It was really difficult for a while, but then one day I thought about how she was when she was alive. She'd be hurt if she saw me the way I was acting. I realized that she wanted me to act like she was there and do something with myself. I knew I just had to get past her being dead. Not forget, but just keep doing what she expected." Yusuf's words came slowly. He continued to stare at the floor. When he finished, he looked up and said, "Those times stay with you even when you don't always act like you remember."

Yusuf's story, although different from mine, inspired me to reveal more of myself. The writing exercise that followed our discussion helped me structure and present my story in a way that was not threatening. We broke into groups of three or four. Bryn said we were to do two things. As a group, we wrote an *exquisite corpse*, which is a group story, with each member contributing a line or two and passing it to the next writer, who contributes a line or two and so on. I teamed up with Elena and Mona. While the writing of the group story was going on, the second thing we did was write of a transforming or significant experience we had had in our lives.

I wrote in short fashion the story my aunt had told me. Afterward, we did another voice exercise and performed our pieces as if they were music. With one person in each group acting as conductor, the rest of the group took directions, starting and stopping their reading, increasing or decreasing the volume of the reading, at the conductor's behest, who also read from her piece. Each group member, when given the floor by the conductor, could read any part of her piece she wished, repeating parts, jumping around, or reading from beginning to end. Everyone could be reading at once, one person could be reading, or any variation of people within the group.

Each group performed for the other groups, with David exhorting us to listen and respond with one's own words, using intonation, volume, rhythm, and repetition. After performing as groups, we came together and did the same thing with alternating conductors. It was a symphony of voices. Some people repeated a line over and over as if they were a chorus responding to the longer, more linear tales of others. My tape recorder was commandeered, and afterward we listened to our performances.

"Listen to that. Listen to that," David said. "That is terrific." He laughed.

I heard my voice on the tape, mixed with others, hard to follow, sometimes drowned out. I doubt if anyone picked up on what I said, but I was talking about something I seldom talked about. I heard my story meet with others', as if they were responses to mine.

Structure is necessitated by community, by being with others, listening to their stories, and finding in them poetry—who the person speaking is—and structure—how the story is told and the desire and courage to tell it. Within a gathering of supportive people, a story has relevance because it identifies a member of the group and helps establish a framework in which the community has significance. Stories assimilate understanding even as they expose possibilities. My story, the fact that I wanted to tell it, was precipitated by other stories I heard, including my aunt's and those at rehearsal that Saturday. During the rehearsal, my story started acquiring structure, started evolving into something communicable. Others' stories acquired structure in the movement and improvisation, transformed into language that spoke for the teenagers and not about them.

THE JOINERY OF OUR STORIES

The multiplicity of stories reminds me of a passage from Cormac McCarthy's *The Crossing* (1995). Billy, the protagonist, wanders across northern Mexico and southern New Mexico and Texas. He meets an old man in an abandoned town in Mexico early in his wanderings. The old man tells Billy that the world can only be known as it exists in people's hearts. He says: "For while [the world] seemed a place which contained men [and women] it was in reality a place contained within them and therefore to know it one must look there and come to know those hearts and to do this one must live with men [and women] and not simply pass among them" (p. 134). This is strange coming from an old man who has spent his life wandering and now lives alone. I suspect the old man sees much of himself in Billy, and although his life hardly exemplifies what he wants Billy to learn, his story is autobiographical.

He ends his story:

> For this world also which seems to us a thing of stone and flower and blood is not a thing at all but is a tale. And all in it is a tale and each tale the sum of all lesser tales and yet these also are the selfsame tales and contain as well all else within them. So everything is necessary. Every least thing. This is the hard lesson. Nothing can be dispensed with. Nothing despised. Because the seams are hid from, you see. The joinery. The way in which the world is made. We have no way to know what could be taken away. What omitted. We have no way to tell what might stand and what might fall. And those seams that are hid from us are of course in the tale itself and the tale has no abode or place of being except in the telling only and there it lives and makes its home and therefore we can never be done with the telling. Of the telling there is no end. (p. 143)

There is much in the telling of any story that is missing, much that comes into it that is unknown but necessary. It is not left out; it makes the story alive and whole. These are the sideshadows of which Morson (1996) speaks. But in not seeing the seams, in not realizing how they are woven together, the bonding of contexts and experiences, we cannot speak as if we know of what the story is made. We cannot know what is and what is not necessary. There are too many voices, and rightly so. We can only speak of what we have experienced and been told by others, and in that a story lives continually, needing to be told and retold and reconfigured because both the tellers' and listeners' lives continue and with that the story changes. The TeenStreet process is one of exploring and expanding stories to invigorate possibilities for each teenager. It is done for creative and agentive reasons, for both project-based goals and lifelong motivation.

TEENSTREET'S CREATIVE PROCESS AND THE USE OF THE PERSONAL

It was significant for me not only to have written about my mother but to have spoken what I wrote, even under such unusual circumstances. David's symphony exercise allowed me to focus on my poetic ear, on the meaning of the story, without being intimidated by structural concerns, such as how it came across to others. David's excitement at the sound of so many individual voices coming together to form a polyphonic story gave a validity to what was said, as if what mattered was not necessarily what was said but that it was said at all. This is an important distinction made in the TeenStreet creative process.

Getting the teenagers to express themselves—verbally and nonverbally—was a primary task for the instructors. Bryn told the teenagers they were Master Poets, noting that the hardest thing about being a Master Poet is remembering you are one. Ron, Anita, and Bryn felt that once teenagers started expressing themselves, once they were uninhibited about expressing themselves, what was said or done, particularly as it related to perspective-taking and interacting, could be explored. In my case, I took stock of my own stories in light of others' stories, preparing to put my own into the world. This was the case for many teenagers, too. Over and over, they plucked experiences from their own lives that defined who they were. And through interaction, these experiences were enlivened and given multiple possibilities.

Ron, Anita, and Bryn premised the writing process on teenagers sharing their writing and listening to what others thought about it. As part of the creative process, the writing exercises were conducive to imaginal interaction, or the creative interaction of words and actions as a way of imagining alternative perspectives by exploring one's own and others'. The instructors encouraged teenagers to use each other's writing and to "rewrite" what others wrote from their own or an imagined perspective. At the same time, they encouraged teenagers to find something in an experience or story that defined who they are, that helped burnish their own understanding of themselves and the world.

PUBLIC AND PRIVATE SELVES

Bryn often spoke of the relationship between a private and a public self, or between that part of us we hide from others and that part we show the world that the world reflects back to us. Although he did not put it in these terms, the dichotomy of private and public self creates a human dialogism with each self informing the other. Out of this dialogue comes a sense of self as a lived "individuality." The dynamic nature of dialogism implies a fluidity between self and world that cannot be accounted for using binary classifications such as private and public self. As a tool for focusing on perspective, however, it was valuable because the teenagers could see themselves as individuals within the world, looking at the world as the world, in turn, looks at them. Perspectives are created through interaction, in the constant "looking" back and forth between self and the world, which is what happens as the writing and movement exercises are carried forward and others are allowed to respond.

During a rehearsal in early November of my second year, after an intense movement exercise, Bryn asked the teenagers to contemplate their public and private selves. He introduced them to the distinction by referring to the movement exercise, talking about the difference between another's perspective of us as we dance or move and our own perspectives of ourselves as we dance or move in front of a mirror. He asked the teenagers to write how someone watching them would describe their movement. This description represents the public self, or how we imagine our selves to be seen in the world by others. Next, the teenagers wrote about how they saw themselves as they moved in front of a mirror. This part of the exercise was conceived as getting the teenagers to reflect on their private selves, or how they saw themselves.

Nearly all of the teenagers wrote physical descriptions showing how others might see them. Most descriptions, however, included an accounting or interpretation of what others thought. Typical of these descriptions was Angie's, who wrote: "She moves so gracefully almost as if she had buttered her feet. And it seems as if each movement represents a step she's taken in her life. With every spin, every bend, you anticipate more and more and more and then she just stops." However, Yusuf, in describing how others might see him, wrote as if he were watching the person who was watching him:

Something's definitely wrong with this blatantly distraught being,
who keeps changing her dance so I can't keep up,
changing abruptly like an unexpected period,
eyes all shut up
face contorted
likes she's trapped in her body house.
But she ain't,
she's just playing the part she feels I want of her—
acting
like she's caught up.
But maybe she just is encompassed in her individuality,
trying to find a dance she can create ten thousand to.
Or maybe she's a drug addict.
Or maybe she's trying to sweat real hard.

When I first heard this description I thought Yusuf had misunderstood the activity. The feminine pronouns make the description appear as if Yusuf is talking about someone else. And, in fact, the description is of a woman as Yusuf sees her as she watches him. Thus, in describing his public self, Yusuf described how another person might respond to him, suggesting that his public self is a creation contingent on how others react to him. Public self is inferred from others' actions toward him.

In his description, Yusuf wrote that the woman is "distraught," "keeps changing her dance [her story, her actions, her responses to Yusuf?] so [he] can't keep up." His public self, in this case, is something tenuous if not alienated from the other. Yusuf is confused by the woman's response to him, unsure of how to interpret her actions and, thus, unsure of his own status or place in relation to her and possibly to society as a whole. Significantly, Yusuf does not assume he knows this woman's thoughts or what she is experiencing. He provides some possibilities as to why the woman acts as she does, one that relates to who Yusuf is ("playing the part she feels I want of her") and others that appear to have no relation to Yusuf (she's creative, a drug addict, or simply trying to exercise), giving this woman an existence apart from what he can know. Yusuf allows for multiple possibilities to explain this woman's actions. He contemplates his public self as capable of affecting others, but not necessarily so, and especially not in ways Yusuf can always figure out. We all may be trapped in our own "body houses" while appearing to be playing some role or part for others. Others' responses arise from their own perspectives—or "body houses," if you will—and we reflect on those responses from our own perspectives.

Other teenagers, too, captured the tenuousness of defining a public self, only not in the way Yusuf did. For the most part, others tried to capture what they saw as their disconnection from others or others' inability to understand them. For example, Sharon wrote this in describing her public self:

Look at her, well, I don't know what she's doing
her movement is kind of like her speech
kinda confused and mixed up
but very complete and well known—
absolutely nothing makes sense
it's all twisted, yet somehow it's right
for her at least.

Does she not keep the same movement smooth and connected because she isn't able or does she just not care? Oh well, she's alone but also she has the others (wherever they are) with her—does she know she doesn't have a partner. Why does she act like she has one—what the hell is she doing?

I think she's not all here
Yeah, she's happy.

Here, the tenuousness of self in a world of multiple possibilities is represented best when juxtaposed with Sharon's private self. She juxtaposes what she thinks others see and what she knows about herself. For most of the teenagers, the private-self writing was more reflective, presenting inner thoughts as opposed to physical presences. In describing what they see in the mirror when observing themselves, the teenagers were more definitive than in the public-self description. Yet they were still contemplative. For example, Sharon wrote of her private self:

My heart, the mirror
damn the mirror
always shows it all
can't hide anything
who gives a shit.
I mean, I'm not alone.
If everyone's heart is a mirror,
they're feeling the same way I'm feeling
and it's all showing just a lot
of honest truth.
We all have some good,
we all have some ugly,
some funny,
some stupid.
It's all good.
Nobody's perfect.
The mirror shows it all.
Let's try and have fun.
Try harder, learn and be imperfect together.
I'm happy.

Juxtaposed with her public self, Sharon's private self appears full of possibilities and capable of many things. The public self doesn't show all there is to her, although the mirror—her private self—knows all about Sharon. From her public self, we learn that Sharon believes her actions do not make much sense to others, but she sees this as normal. In her public-self description, she appears "confused and mixed up," "imperfect," leaving others to ask "what the hell is she doing?" Others cannot fully know her, she realizes, so why should her actions always make sense to them? In describing herself in her private-self writing as full of possibilities, Sharon explains why she appears confused and mixed up to others. She holds out this multiplicity for others, saying she is "not alone if everyone's heart is a mirror, they're feeling the same way I'm feeling." In other words, we are complex beings who at times appear confusing to others because of our complexity. Sharon changed from first-person singular pronouns to the first-person plural, presenting the multifacetedness she saw as part of herself and as a universal human quality, too.

In describing his private self, Yusuf wrote:

I feel like an indicted suspect,
all nappy and proud,
sporting an arm and clenched fist on my crown
and I'm dancing to some beat I've conjured
in my head that sounds like some stuff
off Curtis Mayfield's Blue Monday People,

and in the mirror I'm all up in I see
a familiar face of creed and race, my brother,
but to my surprise he is corrupt and just another one
rushes to bring me down or hold me up.
I see myself, a non-conformer, trying to define myself,
dancing like I'm in some type of ritual,
dancing to bring down my answer from God,
dancing to prove I'm correct and know what my self's purpose is.

Yusuf, like Sharon, leaves little doubt about his private self. He offers possibilities of who he is as he makes clear he is struggling to find out who he is. Comparing the public account and the private account, it appears that Yusuf understands there are limits to what he can know, particularly as what he knows relates to others but also, to an extent, to himself.

Garrett Duncan (1996) calls the awareness of private and public, or inner and outer, selves "a heightened awareness . . . in which the subjective, or inner self, looks upon the objective, or external self, in a self-reflective fashion" (p. 137). At TeenStreet, arriving at heightened awareness begins with the movement and improvisation exercises and is carried over into the writing. In the TeenStreet creative process, as others' selves, both public and private, are explored and interpreted, the teenagers experience multiple possibilities for the same events.

TeenStreet provided an environment for the working out and exploring of public and private selves under the pretense of creating an ensemble performance. Exercises like the one described above helped teenagers distinguish between perspectives and understand that their own perspectives are complex creations evolving from their own place and time and their interaction with others. The stories and experiences the teenagers told or acted out were material for the script. The script's title, *Body House: A Jazz Tricycle*, came from Yusuf's public-self description.

PERSPECTIVE-TAKING AND PROJECT-BASED CREATIVITY

The movement and improvisation exercises introduced teenagers to the idea that meaning is contingent on perspective, that from someone else's perspective one's words or actions can have a different meaning, giving an added significance to the notion of "relooking at" or revising one's own and others' writing. Also important, however, was the contention verbalized by Bryn, Ron, and Anita and explored in all the exercises, that establishing and understanding one's own perspective were vital to responding to others'. With the ever-present goal of creating an ensemble script, the expression of self on such personal levels was made easier because such expression was understood as the basis for creative interaction and performance. The TeenStreet creative process, while premised on the goal of creating professional theater, allowed teenagers to express understanding of the world, to define their places in that world, and to become aware of others' perspectives of the world.

During March of my first year, as the script for *MadJoy* was coming together, Ron asked Donna, an ensemble member whose character was Mecca, a woman living her life in reverse—from death to birth—to create a scene for Mecca's first (last, really) menstrual period. The idea for this scene came after the theme of the performance and many of the other scenes were in place. Lines written by Lisa in January lent a jazzy stream of consciousness to the idea of coming into womanhood. A reference to a woman's first period as being pivotal in her understanding of the world was the seed for the scene. Thus, in creating the scene, a movement and writing exercise came first, followed by the performance theme and much of the script. Only then was Lisa's writing revised to fit the scene. Improvising, Donna "re-created" the event of her first menstrual period and added lines to the script and revised the scene.

In the January writing exercise, Bryn asked ensemble members to take the point of view of characters they were creating. After doing a movement exercise where the characters interacted, the teenagers wrote about their characters' feelings about love or being in love. Bryn asked them to shadow their writing by picking out a phrase or line from what they wrote and building on that line in a quick free write. Shadowing one's own writing was an effort to get at one's thoughts and feelings by reflecting on how one sees one's writing being seen by others. It is re-looking at what one wrote. Lisa wrote the following passage that became, in part, the lines spoken by the chorus in the menstrual period scene developed three months later. (Ellipses are in original; italicized lines were used in the menstrual period scene in *MadJoy*.)

> *Blue darkness like a sudden harbinger of fate.*
> Alone with no cafe's to chit chat or no one to sit and listen to your unloved craziness, but this one guy whose spit smells like butt.
> And . . .
> All is nothing but a banging noise of a sudden cry of agony when everybody committed treason and rape against each other.
> *Everything is blue like singing the blues and you wanna get bombed and fly like a drunken stork.*
> *When my new panties crawl inside my crack and I wanna take them back but I already wore them.*
> *Everything is blue . . . not like the sky, but like a feeling of death when you feel 1/2 sad, 1/4 lonely, and 1/4 happy.* Dark like life without the sun or you, my son when you used to call me sexy mama.

*And I take your head and put it on my chest to remind you what
mother and babies do.*

Now everything is dead like a crack addict in an unmarked grave.
Like all the bodies of everybody who died during the heat wave and my
panties still crawl in my butt.

Then I feel the music.

My heart pounds rhythm and everything is you on a hot summer
day when my stomach growls like an underground devil.

*But then I get sleepy and realism slips under my covers with me
with a flashlight and some crazy book . . . Macbeth or Catcher.*

*And I keep thinking about how much like Holden you are, but
your cap is blue like my life.*

And looking for something is inevitable.

And it's right there like when you first got your first period.

Then I was happy.

*And that was the last time Angels and Aliens visited my head and
told me the truth.*

Lisa's writing conjures up feelings often associated with jazz or blues, feelings
often dichotomous: want versus rejection, exhilaration versus melancholy. It
also gives physicality to such feelings, showing them to be either drawn from
Lisa's life or from a highly perceptive mind. Probably both. The images range
from the personal and private ("rape," "panties crawl inside my crack," "what
mothers and babies do," "stomach growls like an underground devil") to the
public ("treason," drug abuse, a Chicago heat wave that killed hundreds).
There is even a literary image interpreted through the speaker's experience
(" . . . how much like Holden you are, but your cap is blue like my life"). Of
course, Holden Caulfield's cap in *The Catcher in the Rye* is red.

Soon after the rehearsal in which Lisa wrote these lines, Anita or Ron
typed the writing done that day as part of the inventory of teenager writing.
As the ensemble developed the script, Ron pulled the lines and, working with
Terri, Mona, Lisa, and Michelle, the chorus for the scene, created the section
that they were to recite collaboratively. They edited out over a six-week period
all the lines except those italicized. They divided up the lines, saying them in
the order Lisa wrote them as they swayed sensuously behind Donna. All of
this was done without knowing what Donna was going to do or say.

During a rehearsal in late March, the chorus worked with Tony to create
a dance that would get them onstage, positioned in relation to Donna and the
performance of their own lines, and then offstage. The soft rhythm of Ty's
drumming augmented the words.

While the chorus rehearsed, Ron, Ty, Brad, Donna, and I went to the
studio lobby to watch Donna create the scene. Ron had spoken to her earlier

about the scene. Ty watched so he could create a percussion piece. Brad helped write the scene as it developed. I observed.

With the four of us watching, Donna began. She looked around and hesitated, unsure of what to do next. Ty, who had been making drum-like noises with his mouth, stopped. Donna slid to the side of the chair and looked at the seat without getting up. Then, looking up, she raised her hand and took a deep breath. She looked around, her gaze stopping at each of us. She looked afraid and unsure of herself. She again looked at the seat. After repeating these movements for thirty seconds and appearing more terrified and confused each time, she raised her hand and waved it about, saying, "Mrs. Crawford . . . Mrs. Crawford, uh, can I go to the bathroom, or the office. I ain't feelin' good. I need to go to the office and go home. It's my stomach." Brad wrote what she said, I took field notes, Ron took notes on the scene, and Ty watched. As she started to get up, Donna pulled her shirt down over her pants and backed away from the chair, looking down to where she had been sitting and then behind her. She stopped once she had backed out of the circle the four of us had formed and smiled. "How did that look?" she asked.

The lines spoken by the chorus aptly explained the fear and confusion Donna showed. Donna's performance was taken from her life, with the performance and the words now attributed to the character Mecca. The chorus's lines and Mecca's lines and actions evolved in meaning over time, and were cast to fit different perspectives in different contexts. Similar to Bakhtin's (1986) notion of ventriloquizing, the lines and actions of this scene belonged to someone else before finding a place in the script. Bakhtin wrote that "our speech, that is, all our utterances [here, I would include nonverbal actions, too], is filled with others' words, varying degrees of otherness or varying degrees of 'our-own-ness.' These words of others carry with them their own expression, their own evaluative tone, which we assimilate, rework, and re-accentuate" (p. 89). Our actions belong to everyone "out there" for interpretation. Interpretation belongs to us, too. We interpret others' words and actions and make sense of our lives based on how others' act or react to us. TeenStreet takes what is inherent in speech for Bakhtin and makes it a matter of conscious practice, a necessity, really, if we are to be agents in the world.

Mecca's words and actions and the entire menstrual period scene were taken from many of the teenagers' movements and words, including Donna's and Lisa's. But the audience saw everything as Mecca's and was put in a position to "assimilate, re-work, and re-accentuate" it all and, in effect, honor the experiences of all those who created the scene. The scene depended on all these experiences and stories for its richness. There will be a time and place when someone who saw *MadJoy* will recall the scene when contemplating or reflecting on something else she experienced, heard, or read. In such cases—cases that take place every day in everyone's life—Bakhtin's notion of others' words and actions defining who we are and helping us understand the world and revise our own stories, written or otherwise, will be demonstrated.

BECOMING AGENTS IN OUR OWN LIVES

The TeenStreet creative process helps teenagers reconceptualize themselves not only as writers and artists but also as actors in a world where acting on others' words and actions is also an act of agency. The teenagers' agency is contingent on interacting with and understanding others' voices and on exploring possible existences either as characters they created or through imaginal interactions with others' images. These possible existences arise from the teenagers' experiences but go beyond them. In participating in TeenStreet exercises and in creating a script, the teenagers' experiences interact and are interpreted from different perspectives and, thus, create new possibilities. The script ultimately stands apart from the teenagers' experiences as something unique, something infused with multiple voices. The teenagers are creating new culture—new reality.

Ron was adamant about not calling the scripts biographical, although the writing exercises in the earlier rehearsals always drew on the teenagers' lives. He talked about transcending the teenagers' stories and experiences and effusing them with multiple voices. The revision process was an ensemble process, with each teenager's writing becoming the text on which others reflected, even as individual teenagers developed their characters. Once the workshops were completed, however, characters that were created in the movement, improvisation, and writing exercises often became someone else's to play. One's voice was given to another.

For example, Mona's account of a dream she had when she was pregnant, an account she wrote about and discussed, was transformed into one of the three vignettes of the *Body House* script. In November of my second year, Mona wrote:

> I had a dream. I was walking down the street. My tummy was hurting. The people I was carrying inside would not stop fighting. I was yelling at my tummy while walking down the street. People. People was looking at me like I was crazy. They just didn't know it was a riot going on inside of me. The little people was just babies. How could they be so rowdy?
>
> I got on the bus, the babies calmed down. I was calm. Until one of them kicked me. I jumped up and said that's it! I took a knife from my pocket and cut open my tummy. I grabbed one of the babies and started to choke the shit out of him. People on the bus was looking at

me like I was crazy. I stopped, stared at the people, and said what the fuck you looking at. I took a stapler from my pocket and stapled the babies back inside. I looked up and just walked off the bus. Behind me on the bus an old lady said, "You an asshole."

In the *Body House* script, these lines appear near the end of the first vignette, which centers on a young woman pursued by a young man. For the young woman, played by Sharon, it is her first love. Sharon, recounting her dream, speaks Mona's words. Yusuf tells her that maybe she should not remember her dreams, an obvious denigration of Sharon's perspective as unworthy of memory.

Mona had just come through a difficult pregnancy when she wrote the words that would become Sharon's lines. In the vignette, the words arise in a different but related context, built into, literally, a one-act play of deception and confusion between love and sex and its consequences. The characters portray what Annette Henry (1998) calls subjectivities in flux, taking on many different, and often competing or contradictory, perspectives, as they move through a similarly subjective and fluctuating world.

The process of going from Mona's passage to the vignette took four months and incorporated writing, dance, and music from all the teenagers. This process was like the creation of the first menstrual period scene for Mad-Joy and many other scenes and exercises. What ended up in the script was the aesthetic representation of many teenagers' lives, capturing not one particular experience, but a multitude of experiences and the teenagers' understanding of those experiences. Filled with many subjectivities, the "final" product became an object to be interpreted by others.

The process of getting at the essence of experiences gives the teenagers a communicative expertise many had not experienced before. They not only see how their expressions are understood and reshaped by others but also the multiplicity of those expressions. The TeenStreet creative process is about getting at the essence and interrelatedness of experiences and moving beyond them by taking those experiences and creatively imagining how they might have been and can be different.

RADICAL OPENNESS AND DIALOGIC INTERACTION

The urgency to make one's stories come alive in interaction with others depends on a dialogic interaction, a reciprocal web of human understanding, with the life of a story depending on others who will listen and respond. At the core of such interactions is the ability to come to know the world through others, something Bakhtin (1981, 1986, 1990) posits as innately human, as what we do naturally. When those others' voices don't ring true to our experiences, we often choose to ignore them. Yet we have an obligation to listen if only because our own agency, our own stories, depends on our listening to others and their stories. Language, as a mediational tool, is a resource for constructing and communicating understanding and sharing our stories.

At TeenStreet, what Bakhtin conceives as natural is made intentional, is made pedagogical through the purposeful welcoming and embracing of interaction, especially interaction that reveals our differences and our uniqueness. That there is "no alibi in existence" (Bakhtin, 1993)—that we must act and interact—is celebrated and practiced at TeenStreet. The voices of the teenagers push at the boundaries of the mainstream assumptions about them and about literacy use.

As such, TeenStreet uses interaction to inform our writing and writing instruction, as well as our reading and listening. Made interactive, acting, thinking, reading, and writing become contextualized practices. For the agent, understanding becomes a matter of empathy, of placing oneself within the context of others, or of seeing with the eyes of another, as if one were looking over another's shoulder, knowing that one is looking and can never account for all that the other sees and knows. In turn, as writers—as agents—we must feel the breath of the reader—of others—on our shoulders.

4

Discourse and Activity: The Shape and Shaping of Human Consciousness

It is early March of my second year at TeenStreet. The teenagers are in the middle of script development. They spend time at every rehearsal looking at the script and defining their characters' words and actions. They come to rehearsals with character descriptions and walk around as if they're the characters. Today, Ron sends Yusuf and Donna to the lobby. He tells them he wants them to work on the third vignette of *Body House: A Jazz Tricycle*. He asks them to write about their characters in the first person, to describe them, including what they think, their likes, their dislikes. He suggests that they also describe their characters in the third person, as if they were describing someone else.

Donna says she wants to work alone. She goes to the other office. Yusuf has something written he brought from home. He reads his first-person description of a man afraid of the world yet curious. The man talks about his neighborhood and his fear of being thought a fool by friends and neighbors. He presents himself as knowledgeable and experienced about things he admits having no knowledge or experience of. Ron listens. "Good," he says a couple of times as Yusuf reads.

56

When Yusuf finishes, Ron tells him to talk as if he were that character. "Now let's see this person," he says.

Yusuf walks around the room, not saying anything. After thirty seconds, Ron tells him to go with it, to explore the room for a while and figure out who the character is. Ron leaves the lobby.

Yusuf sits and appears to take in everything around him. He acts nervous and stares across the room as if waiting for someone or something. He looks at me but doesn't say anything. He picks up a cap on the table in front of him, looks at it closely, and then sets it back down, smoothing it out so that the insignia on the front can be read. He picks up a script and thumbs through it. He appears consumed by it until he tosses it back on the table. Momentarily, he bends forward and straightens out the script, stacking the papers on top of each other. He runs his hand across the top of the table and looks up. He smiles lightly and touches the script and hat one more time with his fingertips before settling back in his chair.

Ron comes down the stairs. "Try this," he says, and hands Yusuf a piece of paper. Yusuf quietly reads it. It is something he had written during a rehearsal a few months earlier.

"Who is this guy?" Ron says.

"Just someone I know," Yusuf says.

Donna returns and reads her lines. She and Yusuf discuss their characters and the type of relationship they might have. Yusuf says it's hard to figure out what has happened to these people.

Ron reminds them of the twister metaphor that had been developed during previous rehearsals. The metaphor had been used by the teens to describe how characters can be sucked up into a twister, their lives thrown into turmoil. "It's not important what happened . . . anything could have happened. How they responded, though, is what is really important."

Donna disagrees. "Mine [her character] remembers her first experience with love and how it changes her. She is now turned on her ear by little things." She reads through the first few lines of her description, and stops where her character says, "'Small things can ruin your world. The world can change . . . it does change . . .'"

"That's what I mean," Ron says.

"'People looking at her, and they are different to her,'" Donna reads. Her eyes widen, and she does not blink. "'Her mind is going crazy.'" Donna looks at her writing but does not read. Momentarily, she says, "There's HIV, pregnancy, fear . . ."

Ron appears shot through with a jolt of electricity. "Read those as if they're questions," he says, leaning toward Donna. "Maybe, in the end, she is questioning her existence."

Donna nods and takes a deep breath. She opens her mouth to read and then stops. She stands and looks at her writing, appearing to read it to herself. She sets the paper on the coffee table and starts her monologue.

She doesn't speak, however, without moving. Her shoulders sway back and forth. She rolls her lips in and out of her mouth before speaking. She *is* her character. As if on cue, Yusuf stands and gets in front of her. Her voice quivers but doesn't break. Her questions are directed at him. Yusuf smirks, suggesting to me that this is a woman he does not love. His expression of annoyance suggests that the questions Donna's character asks don't mean anything to him. Or maybe he has heard them a million times? This is my interpretation. I feel it in my own body who these characters are. I feel the tension. What happened today will be played out over and over in the coming weeks, always slightly different, at times based on what is already written, at other times rewritten to match the improvisation. The words, however, always come from Donna, as if her body is throwing them out there for all of us.

PUSHING AT THE BOUNDARIES OF WHAT LITERACY MEANS

Sylvia Scribner (1984) writes that "most efforts at definitional determinations [of literacy] are based on a conception of literacy as an attribute of individuals; they are to describe constituents of literacy in terms of individual abilities" (p. 7). She argues, however, that "the single most compelling fact about literacy is that it is a social achievement" (p. 7). While we can't deny the importance of decoding and encoding skills to literacy development, more than skills mastery is involved in learning to read and write. For example, Donna's and Yusuf's use of their bodies to interact with each other's characters and their efforts to feel like the characters they were creating before and as they spoke are striking. This is not something they did when they first joined TeenStreet. Like everyone else, they approached the movement and physical interaction with apprehension and resistance. Nor did they use writing in such ways before coming to TeenStreet, doing things such as improvising then writing, writing then acting, moving and writing, revising others' writing, talking and writing, and so on. They are doing things that at first didn't come naturally, but that now appear to be second nature to them. Bringing forward the physical, embodied nature of literacy, they provoke us to reassess the importance of the body in literacy, language use, and consciousness.

LITERACY AND SOCIAL PRACTICE

James Gee (1990), like Scribner, believes the focus of literacy studies should be on social practices, which leads us away from only looking at reading and writing and even language and "towards [looking at] social relationships and social practices" (p. 137). The descriptions presented in Chapters 2 and 3 are examples of such social practices at TeenStreet. Let's forget for a moment, however, what Gee's statement means for literacy and consider the nature of any discussion of "social relationships and social practices." Such a discussion invokes issues of human interaction and activity, extending beyond literacy as textual practice. Any discussion of literacy ought to begin with these issues because they get at the essence of what literacy does and can do for people. Although individual skills and abilities influence interaction and activity, the interaction and activity themselves define and often create the requisite needs and skills, particularly in situations where an individual's already developed skills and abilities are valued and used to enhance development.

According to Gee, the work of linguists should get at the social theory that underlies language use within a particular context. Social theories ferment Discourses, which establish ways of interacting and doing, including talking, reading, and writing, for all contexts. Acts of literacy are always part of a Discourse context, both defined by and definitive of it. Since individuals move among contexts, such as home, school, work, and various other social and public domains, and private interactions, they are participants in numerous Discourses and, thus, numerous literacies (New London Group, 1996). They adapt to some of these Discourses and, at least tacitly, understand them. Some Discourses, however, they are excluded from, either by choice, force, or a combination of both, for reasons ranging from lack of interest to overt bias.

Gee (1990) contends that individuals are born into a primary Discourse, a "home" environment where they are nurtured and brought into ways of interacting and doing things. Primary Discourses shape individuals' ways of being in and understanding the world. Secondary Discourses "involve social institutions beyond the family," requiring "one to communicate with non-intimates" (p. 151). "A person's primary Discourse serves as a 'framework' or 'base' for the acquisition and learning of secondary Discourses later in life. Primary Discourses also shape, in part, the form this acquisition and learning will take and the final result" (p. 151). Secondary Discourses, in turn, offer secondary frameworks that influence and shape the learning and development of other secondary Discourses and primary Discourses.

LITERACY IN THREE PARTS: AN OVERVIEW AND CONVERGENCE

Coupled with Gee's definition of Discourse, Scribner's three metaphors of literacy provide a comprehensive framework. Her three metaphors are literacy as adaptation, as state of grace, and as power. As three broad ideological classifications, the metaphors are general enough to describe literacy broadly and to account for the diversity of perspectives of literacy, although these perspectives are malleable. Based on my TeenStreet experience, I suggest a fourth metaphor: literacy as mediational means.

Literacy as Adaptation and as State of Grace

The first metaphor, literacy as adaptation, presumes literacy to be functional, used to improve one's academic, professional, and, perhaps, personal prospects. Literacy as such is often perceived as the accumulation of various skills. Most adult and school-based literacy programs are designed along these lines and often fail for this reason. The definition of functional literacy is a matter of debate, changing to reflect societal needs and concerns.

The second metaphor, literacy as a state of grace, is in many ways a metaphor for academic or highbrow literacy, the cum laude of adaptation. The metaphor has evolved into literacy as intelligence. Yet the transformative proposition of literacy as a state of grace is credible only if in using literacy one is given access to information not available otherwise. One may find great solace and appreciation in reading and writing while, ironically, not always comprehending or questioning what one is reading or writing. Historically, the information read and the solace and appreciation derived were religious in nature, thus the metaphor.

Equating literacy with intelligence often excludes people who have not experienced or learned the type of Discourse expected in a particular context, making access to the context questionable. A common assumption is that because of a lack of literacy skills requisite to that community, a person must not be intelligent enough to acquire those skills. Until one learns those skills, he or she is not welcomed into or capable of being a member of the community.

The Nature of Schooling and Literacy as Adaptation

At fifteen, Chau was one of the youngest members of TeenStreet. She came to the United States from Thailand, where her family lived as Cambodian refugees, when she was five years old. She started school when she was six, unable to speak English. Fortunately, her family moved into a community that included many people from her native country, and she enrolled in a school that had a bilingual program. Of this fortuitousness, she said ten years later: "I mean, like, it was great. The people I know, they are, like, non-English speakers, so I feel kind of comfortable and then later I catch up on the English and everything." Chau worked hard and got good grades in grammar and middle school; by the time she reached high school—a large, urban, public school—she had developed conflicting opinions about school. She said she loved school but wished it were more challenging, although it was preparing her for the future by giving her knowledge. "I know it's good for me," she said.

I asked her about writing in school. "Oh, I do it," she said. Noticing, I think, my sardonic smile, she added in a serious tone, "Anything your teacher says in school is worth it."

"Well, do you like to write?" I asked.

She smiled. "No, I was never into writing. I only did it for my grades."

Chau said the English teacher she had at the time gave students topics or sometimes let them choose. Students and teacher talked about topics in class for about ten minutes. Although this type of discussion had never been described as brainstorming to her, when I defined the word, she said that that was what the discussions were like. Then they wrote, usually in class and, if they wanted, as homework. Sometimes they discussed what they wrote in class. Usually they gave the assignment to the teacher, who then graded it and gave it back.

Chau said she did not do as well in writing as she did in other classes; mechanics and grammar presented problems for her. Then I asked: "If you could tell your English teacher one thing concerning writing, what would you tell her?"

"Don't make me write. I don't feel like writing," she said, emphatic even in simulation.

Chau's characterization of her own understanding of education, including writing, illustrates the concept of decontextualized knowledge and its potential power. Decontextualized knowledge is often presented as objective and authoritative. Its potential power resides in the fact that it might not be questioned even by those who are not well served or who are misrepresented by that knowledge. It would be unfair, however, to extrapolate beyond what Chau said to depict her school unfavorably or favorably. But there is enough information here to understand how she conceptualizes education and literacy.

Many of the teenagers at TeenStreet came to the ensemble with similar views of literacy. These views were particularly representative of the teenagers of minority or low socioeconomic backgrounds, lending credence to the belief that these teenagers' primary Discourses are at odds with the secondary Discourse of their schools. For these reasons, they had difficulty adapting to school-based literacy expectations and practices even as they saw this type of literacy as valuable. The Discourse at TeenStreet juxtaposed these differences because such differences were defining features of many teenagers' lives, which became the material for TeenStreet activities.

Literacy as Power

Scribner's third metaphor, literacy as power, is premised on the notion that those who are oppressed can overthrow their oppressors with the help of literacy. Literacy leads to social change. Scribner doubted this correlation, saying it is more likely that the metaphor has it backward: social change leads to literacy. She cited numerous historical examples of social transformations on a national scale to support her position, including Cuba after 1959, the Soviet Union after the 1917 Revolution, and China after World War II. This view of literacy as transformative social agency is embedded in many ways in TeenStreet theory and practice.

Literacy as Mediational Tool

Social transformation is inextricably tied to literacy, not because literacy necessarily fosters social change or equality, but because it fosters reflection on the human condition and offers ways of coming to alternative views of the world. It offers another means for becoming socially engaged. It offers ways of reading the world, and thus, literacy itself is full of possibilities whose manifestations span the many ways it can be used. Literacy can fuel the imagination, which in turn ruminates on possibilities. Literacy can also be used to stymie the imagination. Literacy is not the cause of change, but only a mitigating factor. In trying to understand what literacy can do for people, we need to keep in mind what it has already done, noting the significance others have given it over time and how it has been used in history.

Literacy as power is the only one of the three metaphors that emphasizes the contextual nature of reading and writing. It is activity-centered and mediational, precipitated by social conditions. As a mediational means, literacy as power depends on the activity for which it is employed. It connotes power and agency, which, unlike the other metaphors, are meant to transform the activity and thus the culture or community in which it takes place. Because of the interrelatedness of communities and cultures, the transformation reverberates like a ripple caused by a raindrop; yet, like with a sudden rain shower, ripples collide and break across each other until there is not one distinct ripple but many interacting ones.

Ideally, literacy as power works at a mediational level, asserting no power of its own, but establishing individuals and communities as potentially powerful through interaction. Literacy has the mediational capacity to transcend time and place and Discourse. Literacy's power as mediational tool resides in its ability to make Discourses suspect by infusing them with multiple perspectives. TeenStreet pushes to make teenagers explorers and questioners of their lives; it affects their understanding of literacy use and their actions and interactions outside TeenStreet. It is in this capacity that literacy is perhaps most powerful, when it is a mediational tool helping its user make explicit the ideologies and practices of all Discourses, addressing those Discourses critically.

Literacy development ideally addresses all three metaphors described by Scribner. Each in its own way represents aspects of literacy that are important in use, yet none can stand alone in defining what it means to be literate.

Essential to literacy is its mediational aspects, which incorporates the individual of the literacy as a state of grace with the social of the literacy as power, the private and the public. This coming together provides a window into a broader conception of literacy as adaptation. This conception considers what is necessary to communicate in particular contexts and across contexts, or what is necessary to develop a communicative voice.

TEENSTREET DISCOURSE AND THE EMBEDDING
OF LITERACY WITHIN SOCIAL PRACTICE

About an hour into rehearsal one February Saturday, Ron gave each ensemble member a half-hour to create a three-to-five-minute performance. Karen was told to do something using her violin that involved not making any music or sound with it. Tonya was told to create and sing an operatic song using nonsense words or gibberish. Donna was given a Maya Angelou poem and told to recite it using movement and "a hippie perspective."

Chau, the last person given instructions, was asked to create a Cambodian-style dance. She was to take a story she knew and turn it into a short dance performance. Ron asked me to work with her, letting her use me in the dance in any way she wished. The ensemble members went off to different parts of the field house to prepare.

Chau told me she needed a few minutes to think about what she wanted to do, so I sat down and watched. She began by moving slowly around the room in balletic sweeps and thrusts, stopping after each movement to backtrack and walk through it again. After each movement she stared at the floor, habitually pushing her medium-length dark hair back behind her ears. I thought she was recalling the story and trying to establish what type of movement would best depict what was happening in it.

After five minutes, Chau said, "Okay, here's what you're going to do." I stood up, and she took me by my arm and positioned me in the middle of the stage, telling me to hold my arms straight out from my sides and spread my legs so that they aligned with my shoulders. "You're going to be a tree," she said as she gently kicked the instep of my left foot to get it aligned with my shoulder. "You need to be strong and ready," she said. She looked at me and, smiling, said, "I hope I don't kill you."

Chau said she was going to dance around me and that I wasn't to move. "When I get ready to jump on you, I'll tell you when. I'm going to hang on your arm." She pulled on my right arm, causing me to stiffen it. "I think I can hang there," she said, testing the strength of it, "for a second or two."

I suggested she walk through it first, letting me know what she was going to do beforehand so I could set myself. Although she was about six inches shorter than me, Chau was well-proportioned and athletic, neither thin nor heavy, a good player on her school volleyball team. She began doing the same balletic steps she had performed earlier, only this time moving around me. After about 20 seconds of pirouettes and gently flowing sweeps where she dipped and rose and turned, arching her back and letting her arms move outward from her body as if she were flying, she slowed and began to walk. "Okay, this arm," she said, nodding at my right arm and slapping my out-stretched hand. She stepped back, eyeing my arm.

I braced myself as she wrapped both of her arms around my arm and brought her feet off the ground. My body didn't move, but my arm gave way. Chau hung on but slid to the floor as my arm dropped to my side.

"You have to grab closer to the shoulder," I said.

"Okay," she said, looking at me. She got up and moved around me again, her arms extended outward as if she were gliding but less balletic now. The character she was portraying appeared bent on getting somewhere fast but unsure of where she was going. "Be ready," she said. "I'm going to jump."

I again readied myself. She slowed and then stopped.

"I'm going to jump on your side," she said, taking a deep breath, "and act like I'm choking you." She held her hands out in front of her and made a choking gesture with them.

I nodded. Chau stepped back and jumped at me, her legs wrapping around me as if I were a tree trunk. I pivoted slightly, sliding my legs sideways to keep from falling over and leaning away from Chau so she could get some leverage. She waited for me to stop and then used my extended arm to pull her body onto my hip. Once she was sure she was not going to fall, she put her hands around my neck as if she were choking me. After a couple of sec-onds, she slid off and continued dancing around me, hanging on my left arm and climbing my left side. She finished the dance as she began it, with balletic motion that brought her to the floor near my feet.

I asked her if she had made up the dance or if it was one she had known before. She said she made it up.

"Are you supposed to be a bird or something?"

"Yeah, you can tell, huh?" she said, appearing pleased. "I'm a bird." She flapped her arms and laughed. "A little bird."

"Not a chicken?"

"No," she said, rolling her eyes and clicking her tongue before laughing. "A beautiful bird. Can't you tell when I attack you?"

I laughed. "So what's the story about?"

Chau looked at me, silent for a moment. "Well, it's a story my mom told me before. A lot when I was little. It's a story from Cambodia, about all the wars there and everything."

"So what happens in the story?" I asked.

"Well, the bird is like the Cambodian people, I think," Chau said. "It is afraid and flies around asking for help. He bothers others, pleading, 'Help me. Help me.' But no one helps. The two times I jump on you and choke you, I am the bird pleading for help, begging you. When I fall off, I am being refused and fly away. When I grab your arm, I am trying to rest in a safe place but, you know, I fly away. I can't stay on your arm and rest forever."

"So what happens in the end?"

Chau looked at me. "I don't know. It's not too clear, is it? The bird decides to take care of himself and is at peace. I didn't know how to do that part."

I nod. "I see it now, since you told me. I can see that in what you do."

"In the story, the bird stands up for himself and then others help him."

I told Chau as we rehearsed that she was good at creating dances that told stories. I told her that I remembered her audition performance in October and that it, too, told a story. I didn't know her then, and this was the first I had mentioned to her how interesting and powerful her audition was. Indeed, it was the audition I remembered most, and I was not surprised at the first rehearsal when I saw she had made the ensemble.

Chau's audition combined Cambodian dance with acting out a scene of family life, including dialogue, and ended with her singing a Cambodian melody. The transition from the dance, which Chau described to me in March when I interviewed her as a traditional Cambodian dance step that featured minimal movement, to a scene of family life depicted for me the turmoil and conflict of trying to live within two cultures, in this case, trying to maintain a connection to Cambodian culture while living in the United States. I understood that to be what Chau was trying to convey, although I had not yet met her. In the audition, Chau played all the parts. First, she was a mother working to prepare a meal. Then she was a father, arriving home, drunk and violent, verbally abusing and rushing the woman, arms flying about ready to strike her, accusing her of being unfit, of failing to raise their children properly. The gist of the action was all speculation on my part because the dialogue, or monologue really, since only the father spoke, was in Khmer. Chau later confirmed my impressions. Finally, after the father stormed out, the audition performance ended with the mother on her knees, softly singing, her eyes moist and staring off into space as if she were praying.

In our formal interview, after I told her how much I liked it, I asked Chau how she created her audition performance. The dancing and singing parts were easy, she said. She had intended only to dance and sing. The acting workshop instructor who suggested she audition for TeenStreet told her she needed to create something herself, to write something that showed how she thought. Chau said that she did not think she could do it. "I didn't know what to do," she said.

I asked if she wrote the lines spoken in the audition. Yes, she said, and when she practiced, her acting instructor helped her arrange everything. "I was surprised how good it was," Chau said.

"Where did the writing come from?" I asked.

"It came from things I've seen," she said. "I know a lot of families that act like that. It happens all the time, especially for Cambodians whose kids grow up here. The parents don't understand what it means to grow up here."

CONTEXTUALIZING LITERACY PRACTICE

Chau did not do any reading or writing during her performance for the February rehearsal. In fact, she did not even say anything during the dance. The story on which the dance was based, as Chau noted, was told to her by her mother, and I took it to be a Cambodian folk tale passed on orally. The performance, however, was imbued with elements of literacy use, or with the effects of literacy use. Chau's audition performance, which included writing, and the February performance were defined in part by and definitive of Chau's literacy experiences at TeenStreet and can be juxtaposed with her earlier descriptions of school experience. The Discourse of TeenStreet summoned Chau's creativity in ways that allowed her to use her primary Discourse, and thus her understanding of the world, as a way of not only entering and defining Teen-Street Discourse but also other Discourses of which she was a part. Literacy was used to mediate and communicate her understanding of the world.

I have three reasons for thinking this. First, the February rehearsal performance, and I speculate Ron's idea for the performance, grew out of Chau's audition and affirmed her lived experience and use of literacy to help communicate that experience. Chau's perspective of the world was given prominence in the exercises and seen as a viable interpretation of the world. Second, exercises such as the creation of a performance that involved multiple uses of movement, dance, improvisation, and writing, or what I call imaginal interaction, and that are often mediated by writing, affected Chau's consciousness about aesthetic activity and, more specifically, writing activity prior to the creation of the February performance. Chau experienced writing for a different purpose, or a new secondary Discourse. Writing became part of a larger creative and reflective endeavor, a project-based endeavor. She succeeded in her efforts, not only during the audition but in many rehearsals leading up to the February rehearsal. The non-literacy exercises challenged and transformed her understanding of writing as it was offered in school and described earlier. Chau experienced multiple ways of communicating meaning and understanding of the world, contextualizing writing among these ways. Third, and most important, activities such as Chau's dance creation and other Teen-

Street movement and improvisation exercises called on Chau to tell about her experience. The act of telling enhanced Chau's telling or discourse ability during literacy events by allowing her both to practice narration and to create a reservoir of knowledge. The non-literacy events allowed her to bring prior knowledge to the fore as a source for verbal and written discourse. For teenagers whose experiences with writing have not been positive, alternative ways of communicating, ways embedded in somatic and mental imagery, may allow them to recreate or appropriate primary and secondary Discourse language use as a way to tell their own stories.

The aesthetic activity of TeenStreet Discourse redefined the possibilities of literacy for Chau, casting literacy not so much as an end in itself, something to desire and strive for, but as a means, as a way of doing something where the purpose is all-encompassing, affecting one's whole life. Literacy became a mediational tool, a potentially effective way of communicating Chau's place in the world. This understanding infiltrates other Discourses, both primary and secondary; hence Chau's desire to become a writer only a few months after telling me she wished her English teacher never made her write again. The strength of the TeenStreet creative process is represented in Chau's and other teenagers' desire to continue its practices and thought processes, including literacy use, outside TeenStreet.

THE MEDIATIONAL CAPACITY OF LITERACY

As demonstrated by Chau's understanding and interpretation of her own experience, much of the writing done at TeenStreet is geared toward presenting individual consciousness of the world. Similar to the way Chau's performances exemplified the interacting of aesthetic activities and others' consciousness (her father's and mother's in the audition skit and Cambodians'—a societal consciousness—and also Chau's in both performances), writing at TeenStreet was structured to arise from and support other aesthetic activities in a forum of imaginal interaction. Demonstrating this are the following unedited passages from a writing exercise from early November of my second year. Mona wrote the first passage in response to being asked to describe a story she had recently heard.

> The last story I read was Sherlock Holmes and the second stain ["The Adventure of the Second Stain" (Doyle, 1917)]. It was so interesting because it was mysterious. Like for instance, Sherlock Holmes was trying to solve a case about a document that was missing. At first Sherlock would find clues but they wasn't right. Then Watson would start talking, then the story would speed up. I was in such a hurry to finish. When I

finally found out I couldn't believe it. You would never have guessed.
Sherlock and Watson was finding clues. I tried to figure it out before I
got to the end but everytime I would say a person's name, the clues
would start to change and I would be wrong. It's just interesting trying
to figure out mysterious stories.

After the teenagers read and discussed what they wrote, Bryn asked them to
write a more reflective piece, or as he put it, "Shadow what you wrote. Try to
get at it from another angle." In Mona's case, this meant being more experiential. She wrote:

I had a dream that I was a Sherlock Holmes rapper superlady. I tried to
discover things violently. I was always shaking nervous while exploring.
I chased people while creeping. I don't pay attention to people. I am always curious. I eat, jump, and hug at the same time. I talk and mess
with people. I am powerful because I can fly. I am different because I
can fight with my business mind. I never pace. I got the habit of scaring
people. But one day a twister ate me up. I guess it was because of all
the bad things I did.

In the second piece, Mona appears to internalize elements of the Sherlock Holmes story and recast them within her own life. Indeed, although she
did not stop analyzing the Holmes story, she did reflect on its significance to
her, appropriating the image of Holmes, solver of mysteries, in ways similar
to how Ty appropriated images from his own life in his writing that was presented in Chapter 2. Both writers provide insight into their understanding of
the world and themselves. Mona appears to make connections between herself
and Sherlock Holmes, a literary archetype that few people would associate
with a young African American woman from the West Side of Chicago. Mona
saw Holmes and herself as curious and devious ("creeping," "mess[ing] with
people"), often not attentive to others, of two minds, and so on.

In Mona's second piece, some of her concerns, especially as they per-
tained to how she felt about herself, came out. Underlying these descriptions
was the belief that life is full of mysteries and the need for individual exploration, which for Mona could turn up some bad things, thus her nervousness.
In most of Mona's TeenStreet writing, the theme of flying as a source of
power or release from turmoil emerged. Lines such as the following showed
up in her writing: "I could fly and turn in the sky and no one was there to
bother me." "She's trying hard. But now she's crying because she just can't
rise in the air." "I am flying and flowing. . . . Nobody can grab me." Her writing often evolved from moments of flying and ecstasy to landing and being
faced with reality. For example, in December, she wrote:

> I am going out my door. It's starting to rain slower and slower. I go out and start to dance. Just listening to the bass dance in my ear and face. I feel like I am a dancing raindrop. Nobody can stop me. I am dancing around lots of people. They don't even notice me until I started to splash a little bit. No, I am really dancing. People are so amazed because I'm a raindrop getting into the groove. I stop, pause, start to tap my little raindrop feet. Wondering should I stop. No, it sounds so good that I can't stop. And if anybody tries to stop me I am going to kill them. Splashing and dancing to the groove. Wow.

The image of Sherlock Holmes Rapper Superlady appeared to offer Mona the same power and control over her life that she imagined possible from knowing how to fly. Sherlock Holmes is, after all, a mystery solver who puts lives and society back in order after others have knocked them askew.

Mona's consciousness was given substance in the image of Sherlock Holmes and was presented to others here and at other times during rehearsals. For other ensemble members, it was an image that also hit home, giving substance to their own consciousness, as they reflected on their understanding of Mona's writing. For example, after reading Mona's writing about Sherlock Holmes and Sherlock Holmes Rapper Superlady, Chau wrote in a five-minute free write:

> OK, I got a dream that I was superman except I was a superboy with a SB sign with a heart. Anyway, it starts with a television with no picture on it that I came on and said look out, there are more twisters coming toward the city from no where. I appeared at that moment and you came and got sucked up. I was supposed to fly and save them. I ended up twisting. It was weird but I have to stick my hand out far from my body and if I wanted to come down I would bring it back to me. I was acting confused until the twister got me in between. I ended up chasing them away by a little bursting army of mind.

Donna, reflecting on both Mona's and Chau's writing, wrote in another free write:

> Chasing people, I had a dream about flying Sherlock Holmes, curiously. But I was superlady, creeping to finger out what was sucking up my family. Every time I was scared of something that was sucking up my hugging family. I couldn't believe everything was fighting my family away. I started sharing because I finally found out that exploring the world was violence. I got messing with people and threw my arms,

thinking, up high in the air, but attention more because when looked up nervously, screaming. I got my business mind.

And then, during the last part of the exercise, Chau, after reading Mona's, Donna's, and her previous free writes, wrote:

> Everytime I dream I got this laughing and screaming when I dream that I was mad when my brother got sucked up I believe by a twister. My family and I tried to finger out what was going on with superlady. Why, why didn't she save a brother. I asked her last night up high. I threw a pillow, saving me from detention of frustration. Reality. Mad at somethings that can be solved by other lives.

Through the imaginal interaction of writing demonstrated by Mona, Chau, and Donna, the consciousness of all three was given substance. Ultimately, in Chau's last piece, what were originally images used by Mona became Chau's in her depiction of her own life. She zeroed in on "last night" and her concern for her brother.

The twister metaphor Chau used became popular among the teenagers. All these writers applied the twister metaphor to their own realities, using Mona's consciousness of the term throughout the exercise but transforming the image to fit their understandings. These metaphors appear to capture the enticements of life, both good and bad, that many teenagers face.

These related works represent much of the writing done at TeenStreet. The writing tapped into the teenagers' experiences by being dialogical, allowing them to respond to each other and see their own perspectives opened up and made broader by others' perspectives. They shared multiple views of the world. The dialogical writing exemplifies literacy as mediational tool. It casts the teenagers as active presenters and questioners of their and others' existences.

The Sherlock Holmes Rapper Superlady character took a narrative role in the performance that was created and performed four months later. She spent the performance, along with her trusty sidekick Watson, searching for her family, who had been sucked up by a twister.

Rapper Superlady and Watson moved about the stage during the performance, assuming a chorus-like role. During their search, three similarly crafted vignettes—or three cycles, as the title *Body House: A Jazz Tricycle* implies—showed three different teenagers being sucked up in their own twisters.

Early in the performance, we met Rapper Superlady (*Author's note*: which becomes Super Lady in final version) and Watson, who stopped their examination of clues—scattered debris left by the twister—and introduced themselves and their story.

> TERRI (RAPPER SUPER LADY): I was mad when my sister got sucked up. Now another sister! I will try to finger out what is happening. That's why I became "Sherlock Holmes Rapper Super Lady."
> ANTHONY (WATSON): Who?
> TERRI: I am Sherlock Holmes Rapper Super Lady creeping to finger out what was sucking up my hugging family.
>> I found a clue in the dirt, my sisters were sucked up, I believe by a twister.
> ANTHONY: Let's go find a twister.
> TERRI: Because of my sisters, Super Lady will discover things violently. Super Lady will chase people while creeping. . . . Super Lady is always curious.
> ANTHONY: Sherlock Holmes Rapper Super Lady.
> TERRI: I eat, jump, and hug at the same time. I talk and mess with people. I am powerful, because I can fly.
>> I am different, because I can fight with my "business mind."
>> I never pace.
> ANTHONY: Never. She fingers things out. Sherlock Holmes Rapper Super Lady.

Whether intentional or not, the use of "fingers" instead of "figures" lent a physicality—a bodily image—to the notion of exploration, making it wholly grounded in experience, implicitly suggesting the influence of the movement exercises on the writing.

CONSCIOUSNESS AND LITERACY: A THEORY

Understanding the mediational capacity of literacy requires grounding literacy within a particular context and reflecting on its use within that context. Interpretation of human activity and interaction of which literacy is a part should take into account both the actions carried out by the participants and the interaction among participants. The descriptions of Chau's experiences and the writing of Mona, Donna, and Chau are examples of this accounting. People do things for reasons that, even in doing the same thing, can vary among people. Observations of activities move beyond the behavior of the participants to consider things such as motives and goals, including participant perspective, or consciousness, of the world. (Here and in later chapters, I use the terms *thought*, *perspective*, and *consciousness* interchangeably.)

Most concepts of consciousness presume some type of interaction be-tween the conscious subject and the world. In Western thought, this interac-tion has been defined in the most rudimentary of ways: Humans interact with the world, with humans on one side of the interaction and the world on the other, usually with humans deriving understanding from the interaction.

Leont'ev (1981a), however, believed that "consciousness is determined by people's social being, which is nothing other than the actual process of living. The process of living is the aggregate or, more precisely, the system of activities that succeed one another" (p. 46). Consciousness is formed in activ-ity, including interaction, yet it is more than just an accumulation of under-standing. One's consciousness proffers motivation for the subject or offers meaning and interpretation of one's action in the world. The aggregation of activities forms our knowledge or understanding about the world, which, in turn, directs our participation in other activities and our interaction with other subjects. At the same time, the world—objects, structures, artifacts—is sub-jectified through human action. As the subject's understanding evolves with each activity, the object is defined in its relation to the activity. A subject does not so much interact with the world as it interacts with the conscious representation given to objects by itself and others.

CONSCIOUSNESS AND LITERACY: AN EXAMPLE

In the description taken from the February rehearsal, Chau's bird story came to her as an object, something apart from her and in the world. Her mother told her this story. She interpreted it when she created the dance and pre-sented it to me and others at the rehearsal as an object. Chau's interpretation is imbued with aspects of her relations with her mother and memories of her childhood, among other things. The story is an object that Chau became aware of in a different activity process than TeenStreet's. Her understanding, pre-sentation, and telling of it subjectified it for her, inoculating it with her con-sciousness.

My understanding of the story, however, arose in part from my participa-tion in it and in the TeenStreet activity as a whole. Aspects of this participation included my role as researcher, my sketchy understanding of Cambodian his-tory, and the influence of another object—Chau's audition performance— among other things. My interaction with this object was and my subsequent consciousness of it will always be imbued with Chau's interpretation of the object. For me the object—the story—is qualitatively different from Chau's even as my understanding depends on Chau's presentation of it. This is not to say that my understanding or Chau's or others' understanding of the story will not change. It will, as we involve ourselves in other activities that call forth our subjectifications of the object, whether it be a retelling of the story, the telling of a similar story, or even a dance that brings the story to mind.

The same subjectification takes place in Mona's use of the Sherlock Holmes story and, subsequently, in Chau's and Donna's use of Mona's stories. Mona's first piece appeared to reflect the activity of school as she recalled characters and events in the story, the nature of a Sherlock Holmes mystery with its linear path toward resolution that draws the reader into trying to figure out the mystery, and an analysis of the story itself. Mona read the story as part of a school assignment, and it is not surprising that the "type" of writing she did at school made its way into the writing at TeenStreet. When Bryn suggested the teenagers tell a story that they had recently heard, Mona told one she had read, absent of much reflection although astute in its analysis. The purpose of taking another look at one's writing is to push beyond one's understanding of an object and infuse it with another part of one's consciousness. At TeenStreet, statements such as "taking another look" or "shadow your writing" became cues for doing this. Mona's second piece reflects her understanding of the story in a way representative of TeenStreet activity and its motives and of Mona's own interpretation as it relates to activities beyond school. Mona subjectifies the Sherlock Holmes object, using her covert consciousness—her idiosyncratic and contingent understanding of the world—to transform a traditional or overt understanding of Sherlock Holmes, at least within Discourses common to formal instruction and literary criticism.

Donna's and Chau's understanding of the Sherlock Holmes story, if they read it and made a connection between it and Mona's two pieces, would likely reflect—or as Bryn says, shadow—Mona's understanding. The object—the Holmes story—would be interpreted in light of the activity process in which it was encountered and the writers' consciousness of prior activity processes and encounters. Reflecting covert consciousness is necessary to bring into question the ideology and practices of Discourses. It is also necessary to keep stories alive and viable for others. Stories, like Discourses, live only to the extent that we can enter and burnish them with our own understanding.

THE SHAPE AND THE SHAPING OF CONSCIOUSNESS

Recall the Leont'ev quote about consciousness in the previous section: "consciousness is determined by people's social *being*" (emphasis mine). Another way of saying this is that understanding of the world is mediated by our interaction with it, whether the interaction is with objects or others. All of the interactions described in the previous section involved language to some degree. Mediation, however, comes from many places and objects, including activity and context, other people, our motivation and goals, our past experiences, and future aspirations, as well as language and other sign systems. We are born into interaction and continue in interaction throughout our lives. Yet understanding is a process of internalizing our interactions, of taking what is external—objectified—and making it our own—subjective or internal. Zinchenko and Gordon (1981) describe the process this way:

> Internalization is the transition in which external processes with external, material objects are transformed into processes that take place on the mental level, the level of consciousness. During this transition these processes undergo specific change—they become generalized, verbalized, abbreviated, and most importantly, they become means for further development that transcends what is possible with external activity. (p. 74)

As individuals, we hold sway over external activity, regardless of the Discourse, in our ability to name it, evaluate it, and realize we could have acted differently in any action we take. We draw on external activity, making it part of our consciousness in ways unique. We each stand in the world as barometers of contingency, defining and acting in the world from a particular place and time, which, although establishing each of us as potentially creative and unique human beings able to act from a place and time no one else can claim, also makes us limited to that place and time, unable to act from another person's place and time. Interacting with the world and with others is the only way to broaden one's space and time contingency, to step vicariously beyond our own space and time.

COMING TO CONSCIOUSNESS

Language is not necessary to mediate activity and interaction. Recall Chau's dance performance in which I participated. I understood much of what she performed before being verbally told the story behind the dance. However, the verbal telling made the dance more meaningful for me, helping me organize and confirm my thoughts about it. Language is our quintessential mediational tool among many necessary mediational tools because it is capable of mediating the use of other tools.

Leont'ev (1981b) gives the following example:

> Thus, we "see" a triangle and cognize it thanks to the fact that a generalized image of a triangle is formed in our consciousness. But the very image emerges only as a consequence of operating with direct sensual data and on the basis of the abstract features of any triangle fixed in linguistic form and reflected in the meaning of the word *triangle*. (p. 250)

With the help of others, we learn what the object *triangle* is. We also see triangles, or experience them through other mediational tools. Our experience of a triangle and the mediational means that fostered that experience filter into what we think a triangle is and what we think about a triangle. Our verbal interactions with others confirm or revise our understanding or consciousness of a triangle. The next time we see a similarly shaped object, we are inclined to say it is a triangle not only because we remember someone telling us that a particular object is a triangle but because within our consciousness—within our understanding—there is the concept of triangle.

If in learning about triangles we were shown a three-sided iron object that was clanged with an iron bar to announce dinnertime, we may look at other triangles and although we may not be hungry or even expect to eat soon afterward, reminisce about, or at least be conscious of, the particular triangle used as a dinner bell. It may be what comes to consciousness when we think of triangles. The same thoughts may also arise with only a mention of the word *triangle*.

This example is simplistic, however, for other thoughts may arise in our interaction with a triangle, and it is with this notion that I want to end this chapter because it gets at interaction as being agentive, at Discourses being malleable, and at literacy being invaluable to both. It is this concept that drives the discussion in the next two chapters.

OVERT CONSCIOUSNESS

Because of the distinction that can be made between the "commonly" known definition of *triangle* and the definition or consciousness particular to one's experience, there is a duality of consciousness represented in all people's conception of triangle and, for that matter, most anything else we may think about. On one level there is the usually agreed upon concept of the word or phrase. For example, whether we agree that an object is shaped like a triangle—is a triangle—is not significant; we usually can agree on what a triangle is, at least enough to understand each other.

This understanding I call overt consciousness, meaning it is open to view, often taken for granted, and expected to be understood by most, if not all, people. It is a public or cultural consciousness. And it is aligned closely with one's primary Discourse and those secondary Discourses that one knows and believes represent reality. Overt consciousness gives rise to socially shared or dominant meaning(s), objectified and cut loose from experience and thought and understood without any related real or vicarious experience.

When we understand what others are trying to communicate to us, we conclude that there is a socially shared meaning. What passes between us as communication is often taken for granted as being understandable. For the most part, this is how we function in the world, and for the most part it works, but when it does not, it can be detrimental to our ability to function within a Discourse.

The effect of overt consciousness is that it can close down creativity and initiative within a Discourse. It can make reality static, appearing objective and preconceived, and beyond our influence. Reality appears "natural." Such consciousness leaves one convinced that everything is understandable or known by everyone participating in that context. Ignorance or not knowing, in such cases, is a mark of inferiority. On the other hand, overt consciousness allows for stability and understanding in our interaction with the world and others. It provides norms or ways of knowing that, as noted above, help us coexist and communicate with others.

COVERT CONSCIOUSNESS

Overt consciousness, however, is not the only understanding of the world we enlist in our interactions with others. Our primary and secondary Discourses, and our existence in unique places and times, provide us with ways of knowing and interacting apart from overt consciousness that are often the antithesis of commonly accepted knowledge. Such ways of knowing and interacting, while possibly overt in a particular Discourse, leave other Discourses in duress, pushing at their seams—their joinery—and infusing them with openness by breaking through their boundaries. Such consciousness is covert, meaning it is concealed, secret, or disguised, at least within the context in which it is covert. For example, triangle may have a different, "uncommon" meaning that exists alongside the overt meanings, as in the dinner bell–triangle collusion, or that exists apart or even in opposition or in response to common meanings.

Covert consciousness may arise from the contingency of life and not be particular to any Discourse. In such cases, it is uniquely individual or local. Contingency is perspectival, and covert consciousness is often affectively and physiologically felt by one's whole being. It is seldom only cerebral. Covert consciousness of this type is never fully transferable to others, although it can be shared and made vicarious. It can also be an understanding grounded in the memory of an experience or story that exists alongside or subsumes other consciousness. For example, one's rapid heartbeat and consuming dread following the ringing of a phone because terrible news was once conveyed via telephone represents covert consciousness. Even the mention of the word *telephone*, as in "While you were out, you received a telephone call," or a telephone ringing, may bring on those same feelings and reflections. Addressing the tension that can arise with covert consciousness is a direct addressing of one's own experience. Yusuf, writing in late November, tried to excavate the feelings behind his consciousness while laying out the experience of the excavation itself (ellipses in original):

> I'm slowly but surely learning that true faith is the most difficult thing to possess. It's amazing how a phone call can make uncomfortable feelings resurface and at the same time make you regret that you ever tried to suppress them. (Somehow the uneasiness was enjoyable and fullfillingly miserable.) And now that I have to attempt to deal with them again the effect is so stupidly profound that . . . I'm left alone in this room with my own thoughtlessness and the gentle rhythm of my breathing accompanied by the tick of the clock that seems to mock my dumbfounded silence. To say I'm confused would be both an understatement and a lie—to direct my energy and band-aid my emotions is staring me in the face. Now, I guess the question is whether I will step up and confront it, keep trying to ignore it, or just take the batteries out of the clock.

When covert consciousness gives shape to a different perspective, Discourses collide. Socially shared meaning is brought into question and made debatable. Misunderstanding and alienation can result, but not necessarily. We cannot assume that our understanding, or even how a word makes one feel, is shared by others. We may be better served by assuming that meaning is never fully shared. And although we can continue to name the world, we must doubt our naming as absolute.

TRANSFORMING DISCOURSES

Covert consciousness is not so much a critique of a Discourse as it is a conscious infusion of one Discourse with another. Under such conditions, Discourses are ripe for exploration. The entering consciousness opens the other Discourse to possibilities or alternative perspectives. It is like opening a door and finding 100 more doors on the other side. Not all the doors can be opened, but by opening some, one's perspective is broadened, able to take in more space and time, which may present more doors that need to be opened. In the process, Discourse is transformed.

Because Discourses are always jostling against each other, as Gee notes, there are few "pure" ones. Thus, the distinction between Discourses and even between overt and covert consciousness is blurry. We may use overt consciousness to understand and come to terms with covert consciousness and vice versa. Yet working the tension between overt and covert consciousness must be conscious and purposeful. One must know why he fears the ringing of a telephone and contemplate that consciousness in relation to others. Yusuf questions the feelings that arise with a phone call. Indeed, making people aware of Discourse differences is an exercise in developing consciousness by making them aware, making them questioners and ruminators, of their experiences.

In the example of the Sherlock Holmes story, covert consciousness is brought to the fore in Mona's efforts to weave her own experience with the story, to imbue the story with her subjectivity. In this case, Mona's covert consciousness is used to reflect on her and others' lives and subjugate overt consciousness.

Mona made the choice to imbue Sherlock Holmes with her own life experience and, in a sense, destabilize what Gee (1990) calls the "illusion of lack of agency" that accepts and posits the world as being beyond one's influence. Mona pulls from her covert consciousness an understanding of Holmes and of twisters that are uniquely hers and that inform her own self-understanding and, consequently, others'. Indeed, Sherlock Holmes is part of the master myth, or the dominant Discourses, of the world. Holmes is a model of the modern-day lawman, a hired sleuth with a host of capable but inferior associates around him. He shows no fear or doubt and never makes a mistake or blows a case. Indeed, he thrives on the mistakes of others. Mona turns this archetype on its head in describing herself as Sherlock Holmes Rapper Superlady.

Master myths help form our overt consciousness, "hiding from us ways of thinking, even ways that co-exist in the society with the master myth. They come to seem 'inevitable,' 'natural,' 'normal,' 'practical' common sense" (Gee, 1990, p. 91). Hence, popular culture keeps giving us the same lawman or obviously satirized versions of that lawman. The only way to subvert these myths is by conscious reflection. Literacy is but one way of drawing on covert consciousness and subverting master myths. It has the accumulative ability to influence Discourses over time and space and among multiple participants. Chau did this in her experience at TeenStreet. She learned to work the tension between covert and overt consciousness in creative ways, using other mediational means and language itself to place herself as mediator of that tension. Her first effort at this was her response to her acting instructor's suggestion that she needed to create something more for her audition than only a dance. Her acting instructor's encouragement suggested to Chau that writing can mean more than how it was presented to her at school.

WORKING THE TENSION BETWEEN COVERT
AND OVERT CONSCIOUSNESS AT TEENSTREET

The tension between overt and covert consciousness is evident in the concept of time. Gee (1990) referenced time to show the distinction between mainstream, "master myth" understanding and other Discourse understanding. Gee's example shows time to be commodified by the master myth. It is something that does not belong to those who cannot afford it, such as members of the lower socioeconomic classes whose time is given to others in return for minimal payment.

In the spring of my first year, Ron interviewed Donna, a young African-American woman who lived in a public housing project on Chicago's South Side and was cast as Mecca, the woman living her life in reverse, in *MadJoy*. Since the play was premised on alternative conceptions of time—Mecca going backward from death to birth and everyone else moving forward—questions about time were discussed during rehearsals. Ron began by asking, "What is the shape of time?"

> *DONNA*: The shape of time is more based on experience. . . . Because if you ask me what time is, most people that I do talk to and I already know how to answer this, time is anger. It's bitterness. And time is struggle.
>
> *RON*: What if there is no struggle? Does time stand still?
>
> *DONNA*: If there was no struggle I think I'd be at least halfway rich. Or I'd have a nice house.
>
> *RON*: Does having a nice house mean that time is different?
>
> *DONNA*: Most definitely. Because they [people living in nice houses] probably don't even worry about time. With us not having money we always say, we got to save, we've got to constantly save. And focus on saving. Time for poor people like me is just the main focus more than even living. Time to eat. Time to save. Time to go to sleep. What am I going to do when I get up? What am I going to do if I have no money? Time is hard. I mean everything that comes out a lot of poor mouths is time. "Dag, it's time for me to start saving." "Dag, it's time for me to start looking at things differently." "Dag, it's time for me to grow up." "Dag, it's time for me to change. What am I going to do this time." It's time, time, time.
>
> *RON*: Do rich people not think of time?
>
> *DONNA*: The only thing I can think of a rich person saying is it's time to make more money. We focus more on time than anything. When we have things we don't even think about time until time

runs out. And that's only a little bit. So it's right back on time, I
mean.

RON: How can time be different for people?

DONNA: Time is like the el train [Chicago Transit Authority]. Time's
speed changes. One minute you happy, one minute you sad. One
minute you don't know who to be mad at. To be mad at yourself
or to be mad at somebody else. That's pretty much how time be
changing in our world.

RON: So time is emotions?

DONNA: For some people time just don't go nowhere with them, 'cause
they don't let it. So people with time can go on forever and ever,
like the boys up under my building. To sit there almost like ten
years, to sit in the same environment and do the same old things.
"Damn, don't you get bored?"

RON: How does time move for those boys out protecting your building?

DONNA: It don't. It just stay the same. Forever. It seem like forever. I
mean what could change up under the building? What you see a
different hype [drug user]? That's the only thing that may change,
a different hype coming to buy a rock [cocaine]. I don't see nothing change. I don't understand.

Donna's primary Discourse community measures time by experience, speeding up or slowing down depending on the nature of the experience. For those
whose experiences never change, such as the gangbangers in front of her
building, time stops and the same things happen every day. For those whose
lives are in constant change or movement from having and not having, needing
and fulfilling needs, time moves quickly. Time is packed with emotions like
bitterness and anger. To talk about time is to talk about what is happening or
what needs to happen. For Donna and others in similar positions, life is mea-
sured in time used doing things. (Note that the rich do not do things; they
only make money. For example, they don't make automobiles, build houses,
or produce goods to earn money; they make money, period.) And if things are
not being done or if they need to be done, time is called on as an indicator
of change. For Donna and people with similar perspectives, time is about
living, and there never seems to be enough of it.

When Ron asked if rich people think about time, Donna presented a
different concept of time. Time, for the rich, means money, and since rich
people have money, they probably do not think about time as much as Donna
and others do. Donna named the master myth conception of time set out by
Gee (1990) and analyzed it from her perspective. She decommodified time,
knowing that there are those who commodify it and why.

Donna critically evaluated each conception of time, seeing the ideology behind each. At the same time, she portrayed her and her community's life and their concerns and needs. Her ability to identify the master myth, however, does not let her fall prey to its beliefs or miss seeing the diversity, and thus possible existences, within her own community. As she said later in the interview with Ron, "Things do change." When asked how time is different for her now than in the past, she said:

> Now I'm a freshman in college and it's just totally different. I remember when I used to buy my own [bus fare] tokens. I could just spend my money how I wanted to. I'd be like my mama going to get me car fare. [Now] it don't even feel right asking her for money. So. And I don't know if I'm making it hard on myself because I know that I can get it [from my mom]. I'm making it hard on myself or it is really this hard?

She followed this statement with a story of how her friends have traded control of their lives for allowing men to take care of them. She asked rhetorically, "And what you going to do when he start whupping on you? You dis him or something?" They have given their time away, commodified along with their bodies in a sense, in exchange for being taken care of.

Donna reflected on time for her primary Discourse community and for mainstream society. What made her understanding covert is that she defined herself within her ruminations without being consumed by them. Although she internalized external objects and external processes, Donna also transcended them, grounding them within her experience and analyzing them from her perspective while trying to understand others'. Donna addressed her own existence, but not at the expense of denying others' experiences. Notice also that she is a questioner of others but never made claims for them.

The creative process at TeenStreet strives toward this goal. Allowing covert consciousness to exist and inform overt consciousness opens a Discourse to possibilities and establishes literacy, as well as other mediational means, as sources of power, making all Discourses open to questioning.

5

Reconceptualizing Ourselves in the World as Agents and Experiencers

It is a cold November day of my first year. Ron leads the teenagers through warm-ups, saying little. When they finish, they're on their backs again, staring at the ceiling. Ron tells them to close their eyes and listen to him. "Don't move. Imagine your body is moving." He begins, speaking slowly, pausing for a few seconds between each sentence.

> Think of a scarf coming down through the top of your head and enter-
> ing your body. . . . It pushes down across your eyes and mouth and
> neck. . . . As it unfolds and waves inside you, it drops across your shoul-
> ders and to your pelvic area. . . . Let it grow inside you until it touches
> every part of your body. . . . It's moving you, and as it does it's bringing
> you into contact with others. . . . Let it carry you up and down and fill
> you up, your fingers and your feet. . . . Its movement accelerates and car-
> ries you across the room. . . . Now you're a scarf, moving around as a
> scarf . . . and you swoosh across the floor, . . . brushing against the wood,

against others. . . . But you never get caught, merely an intermingler, sweeping around others, and moving on. . . . Now you're being sucked up and snapped. . . . No scarf should be treated like this. . . . Caught and yanked and tossed. . . . You're caught, stuck on a nail, jammed into a crack.

Ron stops talking. No one has moved. "Let's do Zen Spaces," Ron says momentarily. Everyone gets up and moves toward the wall at Anita's urging. For the past three weeks, Zen Spaces has been the main interactive movement activity, used as a springboard for others.

"Come in when you see an opening," Ron says. Ty is the first to move, followed by Jared. After two minutes everyone is moving across the floor, using geometric shapes to define their actions.

As they begin, I write in my field notes:

> I still don't get these Zen Spaces. Seems like there is a lot of forced
> movement—almost mechanical and rote. Playing off of each other,
> which I suppose is the purpose or one of the things to be learned. The
> movement itself has no coherence or at least I don't see it. I want to
> see a storyline. Something I can interpret. As it is, the movements are
> so brief, the connections so arbitrary that I can't grasp any definitive
> story. There are seconds—instances—where I can read what others are
> doing, where I see a point to it. They don't really seem to be paying at-
> tention to geometric shapes.

When I finish, I look up. The teenagers have been on the floor for ten minutes. Now they lay in a pile in the middle of the floor, legs and arms straddled across each other. It is quiet until Tony lets loose a bloodcurdling scream and jumps to his feet. He shakes Anita, pulling her to her feet. Ron jumps onto a chair that had been pushed to the middle of the floor during the movement and starts shaking it so that it bounces across the floor with him on it. Jim and Bonnie backpedal to get out of his way. Ron starts screaming over and over, "I'm going to puke." All the teenagers get up as Ron and the chair bounce between them. They move in different directions, dodging each other until, as if naturally, they come together in the middle of the floor. They stand together and face me, smiling as if posing for a group photo. They appear to be making light of my presence as observer. Tony runs around the group three times as everyone continues to pose and wave, saying "hello" over and over, the tone changing from a greeting to a question. A couple of teenagers start laughing hysterically and others follow, high and low falsetto voices, until the group breaks apart, still laughing.

Tony, Michelle, and Donna come together in the middle of the stage and

make instrument sounds with their voices. When the others notice, they fall
in behind them, humming. Ron pulls a drum onto the floor and begins pounding on it. Others clap and stomp around the room. Tony slides across the floor
on his stomach, using his arms to pull himself forward. Jared and Sheila start
hip hop dancing. The others are fixated on Tony. He jumps up and points to
a drum, nods his head, and begins pounding away with open palms. Some of
the teenagers settle onto the floor next to Ron and Tony and pound on the
floor with their hands in rhythm with the two drummers. Others grab other
instruments—drum sticks, rattles, bongo drums. They play for two minutes
and stop, except for Tony, who now shakes a rattle full of rice. Ron rolls a
tambourine across the floor, retrieves it, and does it again. He rolls it up and
down his arm.

Jared begins singing a bluesy hymn-like tune that pulls Tony in on har-
mony. Ron moans in the background. Brad is the only one not singing or
making music. He skips around the teenagers, dropping straw pulled from a
broom, enclosing everyone in a circle of straw. Ron yells to find an ending.
Tony and Jared are the last to stop, the patter of rice rattling sounding like a
soft rain shower. Jared's voice drops down behind the patter. "Someday I'll
get home. When will I get home?" he sings until there is nothing left, not the
patter or another note.

After the movement activity, everyone free writes. The images of coming
together for a group photo and the falsetto laugh are the subject of much of
the writing and finds their way into *MadJoy*, with excerpts from many of the
teenagers' writing pulled together to form the following dialogue:

TONY: Lights. Camera. Action. Where the hell is the action! I got to go.
    They all see my camera and crowd around me. They wave hi to
    their mothers and the vapor trails from their mouths and fogs up
    my lens. When your lens gets fogged up, hell, you might as well be
    dead. The best thing to do is put your head between your legs and
    kiss your butt good-bye baby because we just lost both engines and
    we're going down. Who can unfog your lens? Who? Not the damn
    stuff that comes in a neat little, shiny package that's hell to get
    open. Like condoms. Hell no, any asshole with a Polaroid can buy
    that. You need some real shit. Some powerful shit that gets in your
    veins and makes the outlines of these shadows into a beautiful
    man. Sparkle and fade. The flash lasts only for a split second, then
    you're back to where you started, with a dark, foggy lens.
TERRI: Keep your lens clean man. Blind people can only take pictures
    of their lens caps.
DONNA: All of this plays into your subconscious, burning in a place like
    the flash of a fire, until the only thing left is the driving rhythm of

my memory beating its way out. I can see your life stretched out in my memory. Someday you will be the same age and then we'll really, finally be able to talk about it. You must be strong. You must be very strong.

BRAD: You have no idea how difficult it is to live with someone who knows what you're going to do all the time. I'd run away from home as a teenager and my mom would always know where to pick me up at the end of the day. When Mom was 35 she was always warning me about "upcoming troublesome memories." But that never stopped me from making those "troublesome mistakes."

In the scene, all the teenagers except for Tony, Donna, and Brad huddle at center stage. Donna, off to the side, is Mecca. Her son, played by Brad, lives an ordinary life, getting older as his mother gets younger. Tony plays a chorus-like, clown-like old man—the caricature of a news reporter. Terri, a member of the crowd surrounding Tony, speaks like a child. The scene carnivalizes the camera's influence on us and the blindness (fogged-up lens, lens cap) of those on both sides of it. Not even drugs can cure the blindness. Amidst all this are Donna and Brad. Donna tries to convey her understanding to Brad and Brad recalls his mother's influence, but neither talks to each other, staring instead into space, with Tony and the crowd around him moving in to enclose Donna in their circle. The scene ends with the crowd spreading across the stage, Donna at the center looking afraid and nervous. Facing the audience, the teenagers begin their falsetto laughing. It continues for a minute until Donna joins in. The laughter continues for another two minutes, pulling some audience members in while leaving some appearing squirmy.

THE BODY AND LANGUAGE

TeenStreet writing activities are grounded in the movement and improvisation activities and transform the teenagers' understanding and use of literacy. As the previous description shows, these activities help initiate and foster an exploration of language and literacy use as mediational tools that arise from and are contingent on experience, even as these tools help define experience.

Roy Fox (1994) contends that literacy education tends to promote "word before image" (p. 6), making language the medium for studying, communicating, and assessing knowledge in nearly all subject areas. In any discussion of writing, language use, even if only implicitly, is usually the focus of attention and seems to matter most. But how often have we tried to put into words that which we experienced or that which we thought, and have utterly failed or fallen short? Relying only on language limits one's range of creativity and inhibits expression and understanding. Our failures to verbalize that which we know and experience do not negate those thoughts or experiences. Our failures may hinder our interactions, which shows the importance of language, but those thoughts and experiences still fuel our actions and interactions and thus our understandings even as we cannot verbalize them.

THOUGHT AND IMAGERY

To transpose Fox's assertion, "word before image," to "the image before the word" and continue to reach backward to the root of that image, we could say, "action precedes images, which lead to the word." The opening vignette captured this process, as the teenagers went from enactive and somatic imagery to visual imagery to verbal, each overlapping and informing the other. The word, or language, was a polyphony of voices, each arising from individual bodies, yet never fully defined or closed off from other voices, being informed by and informing those voices. In this scenario, action—the experiences of the actor—was the foundation of language use and interaction.

The teenagers, individually and as a group, were "meaning weavers" (Britton, 1993). They sorted out and made sense of multiple experiences. In this activity, their bodies were the looms. They took disparate information and wove a tapestry of understanding that carried with it particles of their existence, including their affective and moral, as well as cognitive, being.

Concerning imagery, Susan Aylwin (1985) defines visual imagery as spatial. It concerns itself with what is observable, metaphorically, as a "picture in the mind's eye." Such a picture takes shape in the movement activity as teenagers make sense, first, of the movement, then of others as they begin to interact. Enactive imagery concerns itself with this interaction, particularly somatic action, motivation, and affect. It concerns itself with "getting things done" by drawing on scenarios or stories that can be infused with multiple possible actions. Both visual and enactive imagery are embedded in experience and can seldom be fully translated into language. However, perceptions of time and place, which are important to visual and enactive imagery, are shared and understood through language use. The language ascribed to visual and enactive imagery is like blinders placed on a horse, focusing on particular aspects of an experience much as a horse's vision is narrowed for purposes of control. Language, so important to our understanding of the world, can never fully describe visual or enactive imagery because language, as a mediational tool, is universal. It bridges experiences and points to commonality and differences. The teenagers' words during and after the activity described at the beginning of this chapter captured only a small part of the action and the experiences of only a few of the teenagers. Visual and enactive imagery are idiosyncratic, rooted in place and time and arising from the body, from experience.

The use of somatic image-making, of the body in movement, particularly when that imagery interacts with others', or when two or more bodies aesthetically move and respond to each other, contextualizes experiences as social and focuses on the body as the site of meaning-making. Meaning is not given away, from one being to another, as can be the perception with language use, but is found in each participant observing and interacting through movement. Meaning is contingent on where a participant is in relation to others. The world is imbued with contingency, and possibilities.

TeenStreet activities represent a transactional approach to text and context. Meaning does not so much reside in the words and in the world, but in the interplay and use of words between speakers/listeners or writers/readers, just as meaning, while residing for each of us in our individual bodies, is born in the interaction of bodies in place and time. The fact that interactions are processual, involving multiple perspectives, opens up possibilities. Meaning, thus, while residing in the body, is formed in the space between bodies, where lives interact. Because we never stand in one place and because we are temporal beings, as the movement and improvisation activities demonstrate, meaning is processual and language, malleable.

Visualization Activity

The teenagers' eyes are closed. They are scattered across the stage in standing positions. Ron tells them to begin creating an animal in their minds and letting it shape their movement. "Think of an animal. The animal you are. What animal do you feel like?" He says to start with the feet and move upward to the head. "Take it on physically," he says.

After Ron describes the activity, everyone is quiet. Most of them have their heads bent slightly forward, and their arms hang alongside their bodies. Some rock easily on their toes or the balls of their feet. After five minutes, Ron says, "How does your animal rest? What's he look like when he's just resting?" The teenagers settle into positions of their animals at rest. Most of them drop to the floor and lay still, legs and arms sprawled in different directions. Ron opens his eyes, looks around, and then settles to the floor, too.

"How does he move?" Ron asks. A couple of teenagers jump back to their feet; the rest rise to their hands and knees, their necks bobbing up and down and their butts swaying. After a couple of minutes of acting like their animals, Ron says, "Take a look at your animal. How does its feet look?" After about 30 seconds, Ron begins moving up the body of the animals. "How do the legs look?" He gives them about a minute to experiment with each part of the body—stomachs, backs, arms. "Does it even have arms?" he asks. "Neck."

"Head." "What are its insides like?" he asks. "How does it feel?" All the while, the teenagers continue to move around as their animals.

"You're the animal," Ron yells, jumping to his feet and stepping out of his animal to watch the others. "Remember the jaw structure," he says, rubbing his hand around his own jaw and twisting his head sideways. "Animals have different jaw structures than people."

"The face, hands. How does it walk? Concentrate on how he acts." Suddenly, as the teenagers crawl or bounce around, Ty playfully attacks Jim, growling and sending other teenagers scurrying away from him. They continue moving around, increasing their interaction as they nudge against one another, pushing with their heads, slapping gently with their paws, and leaning into one another. Those animals that act vicious are left alone by others. Before coming face to face, animals circle each other.

After five minutes, Ron tells them to go in reverse and to come out of their animals one step at a time, starting with the head.

The Flame Dance

The teenagers have completed warm-ups and are on the floor, staring up at the ceiling. With only the sound of their breathing audible, Ron says, "Imagine you're a flame." He speaks slowly and evenly. "You're a flickering, churning, popping fire that is growing, that can do anything. Like a fire, you flicker to life from nothing but a small ember maybe. You spring to life in fits of energy."

The teenagers begin to move, coming up off their backs, appearing to be pulled up by their arms and head. Some come all the way up to their knees and then fall down. Quick movements to the sides or upward are like the snap of a sudden burst of fire. Arms fling about, and every once in a while a leg pops up and then crashes to the floor.

Elena and Denise move close to each other. Terri moves off to a corner, where she clings to the wall, her hands sliding up and down it. "You're fire, and you're body is lighter than air," Ron says. He bounces to his feet and, swaying his torso and jumping over others, says, "You defy gravity. Fire can do that. It can do anything. Go anywhere. Your whole body is fire, jumping, bouncing, dancing where you please." Some are standing and bouncing around, while others stay in one place and flicker, using their outstretched arms and bodies to fan the fire of others.

Some of the teenagers come together. Yusuf encircles Chau with both his arms and then spins away from her for a second, returning to hop around her as she stays in one place. Donna joins in, and the three of them form a circle of colliding bodies and flailing arms. They move around the room, engulfing others, forcing them into the middle of the circle they have formed and only letting them out to help enlarge the circle.

After a few minutes, Ron says, "The oxygen you thrive on is disappearing, it's drying up and is gone." Immediately, teenagers begin to slow down. The circle, which now includes all but two of them, starts to fall apart. People fall away one by one, some spinning out of control, others falling to the floor. Chau falls and starts coughing. Ron appears to pick up on this and says, "Now you're a sputtering, choking flame on the verge of dying, a mere spark ready to go out." Everyone slows and settles back to the floor.

Just as it appears that everyone will come to a complete stop, Ron says, "But you fight for your life. You're smoldering, but an ember comes back to life. A strong wind blows life back into you. Your lifeline returns, oxygen slips in and snaps you to life." Yusuf is up before anyone else. He goes around trying to get the circle together again. Most of them join in, but a few dance away, spinning along the walls and rolling across the floor. The circle breaks open and stretches outward and around the stage like a snake, bending back upon itself and breaking apart.

VISUAL IMAGERY AND THE BODY IN TIME AND SPACE

Aylwin (1985) describes visual imagery as being important to the construction of social persona, which is manifested in the perceived appearance of oneself "in the eyes of others" (p. 56). Within the social environments of day-to-day existence, one's feelings about oneself are created in mediation with others. TeenStreet activities try to dissect those feelings, addressing how one believes others perceive her apart from how she perceives herself, the private self.

In the visual imaging done at TeenStreet, particularly in the movement and improvisation activities, the environment one places oneself in is not the sociocultural context of daily existence, à la Aylwin, but one of the teenagers' creation. The environment is the physical body, the self, where the responsiveness of the self is not directed toward others but toward the body. Thus, visual imagery takes on a meditative quality as preparation for interacting with others. The meditative quality, however, does not stop with the visual image; it is played out in movement. Teenagers reflect on their somatic image-making, creating visual images of the self. The visual imagery of the self is grounded in one's own time and place, in one's own being, and becomes answerable to itself. The answers are not found in the visual stimuli of the environment or in how others see a person but in the person's own physicality. Although this visual representation does not align with the environmentally dependent representation defined by Aylwin, it is a similar concept. The self is still a body of attributes that it self-evaluates. At TeenStreet, the focus is on those attributes themselves and their place within the body. Such images are the stuff of warm-ups and pre-interactive movement, where Ron exhorts teenagers to concentrate on their bodies.

During the movement activities, a participant often establishes a rhythm where everything feels natural, where everything flows and one is focused completely on the self of the interaction. Denise, a dancer, saw the rhythm as similar to the feelings she gets when dancing. "You feel a fluidity, really smooth," she said. However, it can happen that while moving a participant can lose the rhythm or flow, particularly when interacting or changing from one interaction to another. Denise contrasted this loss with dance, too. She said she felt awkward during these times, more so than when dancing. Such awkwardness, something I experienced myself, is a result of the focus being pulled from the body to the world around you. One purpose of the movement activities is to work through these awkward times, to stay aware of thoughts, feelings, and movement, and their influence on the body. The individual movement or "small mind activities," as Ron called them, evoke visual imagery and are meant to minimize the awkward times by allowing one to stabilize the self if only momentarily in a dynamic world.

In *An Experiment in Leisure*, Joanna Field (1937) described the significance of visual imagery. She recounted her lifelong exploration of self, including her efforts to excavate the images of her life that continually reoccur regardless of how old or out of place they are. She called these images "inner facts," which were marked by "a warmth and certainty" (p. 53) in her body. She wrote that the imagination uses mental images in two ways: one, as "wish fulfillments," a means of evading hard facts; and two, as a way of thinking about hard facts, as an instrument, not for evading the truth, but for reaching it (p. 50).

Although she described her journey as a meditative one and not one evoked by somatic image-making, Field wrote of the effect these images had on her body. She described the feeling she got from turning inward as a "goodness," like "a cat lying in the sun" (p. 53), although most of her meditations were on what she considered to be "bad" thoughts and "rebellious" or "utterly fantastic" ideas (p. 52). She perceived these thoughts as socially unacceptable, against the norms of society, or, I suggest, as covert. Yet, Fields wrote, in exploring these thoughts, in facing that within her which was "other" than whom she appeared to be, she felt good. She described her exploration of these "inner facts" as making "direct contact, facing 'something,' which is I think inside me, without words or purposes or protection, a direct touching of something which feels like a raw experience of being alive—coming face to face with something inside you, something intensely living—but it's certainly not 'thinking about' something inside you . . . " (p. 53).

Inner facts, when juxtaposed against the seemingly "hard facts" of the world, lay one open, and, as Field noted, one reaches the truth of who one is. This exploration is conducive to "reflective intervention" (Bruner, 1986) of how one might be perceived by others. It prepares one for meeting the world and, in the case of TeenStreet, for interacting. The "small mind" activities help in this preparation by turning one inward, bypassing the use of language or grounding language or speech as arising from bodily actions. As Field wrote of her exploration, it required me "to sink down, out of my head, and into a deeper part of my body" (p. 53).

ENACTIVE IMAGERY AND AGENTIVE POTENTIAL

The visualization activity and the flame dance, like the wave and scarf activities, were starting points for teenagers to enter the third of the image-creating structures described by Aylwin. Enactive representations are where the snapshots of one's life, the visual images, begin to flow forward into the future, into interactions and possibilities.

Zen Spaces

Ron speaks of the notion of self-directing, of playing off another person but doing your own thing. It is a matter of reading others' actions, interpreting what you see, and responding based on what you think and feel. You accept others' actions as honest and respond in your own movement.

The teenagers have just completed 40 minutes of movement activities and are still on the floor. They are breathing hard, unable to stand still, panting and pulling at their clothes, trying to get air into warm bodies. A few walk off to the side and grab shirts from chairs to wipe their faces. Coming out of the activity, Ron moves quickly to the next.

"Zen Spaces," Ron says, as if recalling an old friend. He moves to the middle of the floor. "It is a movement activity that allows you to tell a story about what you see. It is self-directing and requires the honesty I talked about earlier." He looks around. The teenagers have circled around him. Repeating the theme he had introduced at the first rehearsal, he says, "Don't be judgmental in this. Don't judge. Just experiment."

Ron says Zen Spaces is an activity they will do often. Along with Donna, he demonstrates the movement, telling them as he and Donna do it to use geometric shapes when moving. "Use the whole floor and all of your body," he says. "Different parts of the body can be moving at the same time and at different speeds." He walks quickly in a circle, bending his arms across his body slowly. When he stops, he points at Donna, who is moving her arms at a slower rate with longer extensions across her body. "See how I moved my arms? I was playing off of Donna. Reacting to her." He looks around. "Remember tempo. Tempo expresses emotions. Move as you please, using the geometric shapes, like circles, squares, ovals, lines, triangles, octagons, and whatever else there is. Just keep your perspective open."

Ron tells everyone to spread out. As they do, he says, "Use your peripheral vision, and look for possibilities. When you see an opportunity to do something, do it."

The more experienced members like Ty, Nancy, and Donna go right into moving and interacting. The newcomers move slowly, looking around as if they are standing at a busy intersection with strangers all around. They imitate the more experienced members, following them and playing off their movement.

Jared, a new member, is alert to everyone's movement. He moves quickly, head up, body alive and fluid. He exaggerates others' movement. When it appears as if the others are ignoring him, he moves in front of them, demanding to be seen. He moves on if he doesn't get a response.

Ron senses that many are uncomfortable. "Don't judge," he says.

Zen Spaces becomes the most used movement activity of the rehearsals. The Watusi activity, where one responds to someone else's movement, is a spinoff of Zen Spaces. It represents the freedom of movement and response that Ron wants the teenagers to appropriate in all their actions. The purpose of Zen Spaces is not to teach teenagers a way of moving, as if it were a dance step, but to help them realize the possibilities of movement. The activity, like all of the movement activities, pushes at the boundaries of creativity, forcing the teenagers to interact and respond.

Character Geographies

Bryn takes over for Ron after an hour of intense movement activities that started with the wave activity. He talks about building characters in our movement. The last couple of rehearsals had the teenagers create characters and either move like those characters or write about or from those characters' perspective. "Characters need to grow from the inside," Bryn says. "Ask yourselves, 'Who is this character on the inside?' Consciously try to figure that out." As he talks, Ron, Anita, and I spread laundry wrapping paper—fifty-foot rolls of three-foot-wide heavy white paper—across the floor, going from wall to wall and taping the ends down.

Everyone comes together in a circle in the middle of the floor. Anita and Ron hand out colored markers. Bryn tells the teenagers that when the music starts they are to walk and talk as their characters. When the music stops, they are to stop where they are and write their reflections—their characters' reflections—on the laundry paper. Begin with the feet, Bryn says. "What is it about the feet that defines your character?"

Ron starts the tape. It's Duke Ellington. He turns it up full blast and then eases it down a bit and laughs. "That should wake up anybody who isn't awake." Off everyone goes, including me. After a minute, Bryn stops the tape, and everyone settles to the floor. "Write about the feet of your character," Bryn says. After another minute, we are up and the music is going again. This time Bryn says to focus on the legs of the characters.

The music stops, and we write. Next are the hips, then the waist, butt, belly, and spine. "What do you call your spine?" Bryn yells over the music. Every time the music stops, we drop to the floor and write. The floor is eventually covered with writing. The paper begins to rip in different places. Anita and Bryn tape sheets back together.

Bryn tells us to "try and run into someone else's writing and connect with it. Take off from there." We drop to the floor and read the writing that is closest to us. The first thing I see is about the chest. It says: "It can provide food for babies and pleasure to men. It can cause strain on your back."

When the music starts, we move on to the face and the head. Finally, we are the whole body of our characters. "Start having more interaction and figure out who you're talking to and what's going on," Bryn says.

We write our last lines. While others are writing, I start reading. Someone had written: "I'd rather show you my piggy back with its ridges and cracks than expose the heart I'm rumored to have. I don't know if it's passion or if my passion is just an act." I try to read everything I can.

"When you finish," Bryn says, "crawl to some writing next to you and see how your character would react to that. After that, crawl to another place." During break, I help Bryn, Ron, and Anita roll up the paper. After break, the writing activity continues with everyone setting their characters in a scene and writing what is happening to them.

FINDING THE VOICE IN THE BODY

In comparing the three structures of thought—verbal, visual, and enactive imagery—Aylwin (1985) wrote:

> Enactive imagery lives by its wits in a way in which the other two modes of thought do not. Verbal thinking provides a taxonomy as a stable backdrop to particular roles. Visual thinking provides an only occasionally fickle social environment, and where available, a vast and infinitely accommodating natural one. Enactive thinking presents only a future, which demands of us that we make it real. It provides an ontological place where we may put our feet up and opt out of

becoming for a while. This relates to the fact that enactive representations cannot be detemporalized in the way that other representations can, to form part of the construction of an objective reality. (p. 170)

Enactive imagery is focused subjectivity, an ontological view of the world as evolving. In enactive imagery we are watching the world in its becoming from the vantage point of ourselves as actors and experiencers. It is an artist's perspective in that life is dwelled upon and (re)played out in one's mind. Yet, in the playing out, we do not know what is to happen next and only from a limited perspective know why what has happened has happened. We see ourselves in the happening and know the world because we participate in it.

At TeenStreet, enactive imagery is represented in the "big mind" activities, or the taking of "small mind" into the world, where it responds and is responded to. The somatic imagery of the movement evokes the progressive nature of enactive imagery. This imagery is fundamental to the TeenStreet writing process, both fueling and lending a bias to it. The teenagers become aware of their own particular times and places and address their and others' lives—concerns, desires, interests, experiences—from their own perspectives. Linda Brodkey (1996) calls this approach to literacy "writing from a bias." Enactive imagery is living from a bias, being acutely aware of our own perspective-taking and meaning-making capacity in the world.

One January rehearsal from my second year was representative of most of the rehearsals after the first two months of both years I was a participant-observer. By that time, after two months, the teenagers were familiar with the movement and writing and there was less focus on the nature or purpose of the activities themselves. An activity tended to extend over the course of the entire rehearsal and included movement, improvisation, discussion, and writing in an effort not only to draw on the teenagers' experiences but also to interpret aesthetically their own and others' experiences.

Like all rehearsals, this one began with a 20-minute warm-up that started with all the teenagers on their backs on the floor. During warm-ups, Ron spoke quietly and slowly, working along with the teenagers and imploring them to focus on their bodies and how they felt. Ron told the teenagers to listen to the sounds of their breathing and explore the pitches and rhythms and the changes in sound that resulted.

The voice activities stressed the physicality of voice, that is, of voice being a product of air moving through the body and causing bodily vibrations. These vibrations underscored the fundamental need of a body, of being, to have voice, to make sounds and use language. David Schein introduced many of the voice activities during an earlier rehearsal. However, Ron and Anita always stressed listening to the sounds one makes when breathing.

Ron told the teenagers to momentarily imagine the room as something other than a theater stage. He said to give it a color or an emotion, something like blue or anger, meaning what emotional effect a totally blue room would have or what a room filled with anger would be like. Everyone was quiet. Ron was creating a scenario for human action and interaction that the teenagers would define based on their experiences. "When you get that image in your head," he said, "let it wash over you and start shaping your movement."

No one is ever told how to act or what to do. The initial focus is always on how the teenagers feel and what they think, so much so that they are asked to keep their eyes closed, concentrating on themselves and not each other. Recognizing that the context itself affects the feelings and thoughts of the teenagers, Ron and Anita suggest that those feelings and thoughts, too, should be explored and expressed in the movement. For example, noticing that Mona was upset and thinking it was with him, Ron told her during one rehearsal to show him how mad she was, to use that anger in the activity and not let it inhibit her. Ultimately, the teenagers should—and usually did—become comfortable with the activities. When this happened, such as the case with this Saturday's rehearsal, particular thoughts and feelings were explored, making way for the teenagers to bring their experiences or their feelings about experiences from outside TeenStreet to bear on the activities.

The teenagers are thinking about how they feel and what it is that is happening to their bodies as they move. They are turning somatic image-making into visual and enactive imagery. For example, suppose a teenager drops his right arm across his body and bends to grab the instep of his left foot. His eyes are closed, and he does not know where he is in relation to others. He may as well be in a completely dark room. He moves fast enough that he knows if he grabs his instep forcefully enough he could knock his feet out from under himself. This image conjures up feelings of losing control or of being knocked down by something or someone else or both. The somatic image of the body brings forth an image in the mind of the body in action, which includes motivation, emotion, thought, and consequence. A scene or event is played out. His thoughts and feelings, while focusing on himself, may be chock-full of other people and of things that have happened to him and others. Maybe such a movement causes the teenager to remember an experience where something similar happened or an experience where the feelings were similar. Maybe what caused those feelings is different than what is happening now, but at that moment the teenager hones in on how he feels and why. He hones in on his consciousness, including the influence of his body on consciousness and vice versa. But as soon as he grabs his instep, the teenager lets go and swings his left leg backward so that the momentum brings his body around in a 180-degree turn, his right leg pivoting below his body. As his left foot comes to rest, everything, including his momentum and feelings, makes him think of running. He is poised to take off. The teenager's body responds to how he feels, and in turn, consciousness is shaped, driving the movement, feelings, and thought along.

In moving, people came in contact with each other, and the contact was a stimulus from outside the body that could make one aware of possibilities. As the teenagers came into contact, the movement was transformed into a "big mind" activity. Everyone's eyes were opened. In a big mind activity, individuals are aware of their environment and respond to it, doing so, however, by acting from their bodies, from their emotional states, which the little mind activity has made them aware of. Big mind activities necessitate a response to others, and thus foster awareness of others in space and time.

Sharon and Denise came into contact, lingering for a moment and then following each other across stage, touching each other on the arms and hands. When Sharon stopped and faced her, Denise spun away and crumpled to the floor. Sharon took off. Denise stretched her arms and legs across the floor, raising her body just enough to slide sideways and take refuge among the legs of the other teenagers.

Ron rejoined the movement and said, "Whatever you're working on, flavor it with blue. Explore blue. What does blue look like, feel like?" The activity became improvisational, a role-play, where the role one took on was an emotional, conditional state. The music settled into a softer, looser rhythm, less pulsating, and the movement became muted, almost stilted, as if boundaries had been put on the extension of the bodies. When people came into contact, it often was marked by quick bursts, as if they were drawn to but immediately repelled by others and moved away, surprised by the contact. Ron often described the big mind activities as focusing on the entire room. "Imagine what's going on all around you." It was hard for me to tell what blue connoted, but it obviously meant different things to different people.

Some of the teenagers nearly stopped moving, appearing to withdraw into themselves. Tonya and Terri tried to turn away from everyone, with Tonya running from one side of the stage to the other as other teenagers approached her. She moved quickly, making sudden stops. Yusuf spun around as if he were trying to see if anyone were behind him. Whenever anyone came near him, he became calm and secretive. Denise got off the floor and twisted along the wall, then settled back on the floor, pulling her body across the surface with outstretched legs and arms as others stopped to watch or jump over her.

After a few minutes, Ron stepped off to the side and watched. Over the past month or so, as the teenagers became less conscious of how they looked to others and the movement activities took on a quality of play, Ron had become more of an observer. He let the teenagers interact, only reminding them once in a while to respond to or be aware of what was going on around them.

Creating a safe place to explore mental images is fundamental to Teen-Street's success. The teenagers, through movement and improvisation, are creating "untrue" situations, situations that, although imbued with real-life concerns, are still separate from their lives outside TeenStreet. It is as if they came to TeenStreet to reflect on their lives but once there are not faced with the concerns they face every day in their homes, communities, and schools beyond reflecting on them.

"When you find a place that seems appropriate," Ron said, "start talking to yourself, start your character and interact. Create relationships with others." The characters he referred to are people the teenagers had been working on in the movement and writing of past rehearsals.

Some of the teenagers began talking, mostly to themselves; others began responding to what they heard, sometimes verbally, sometimes gesturally. Ron moved across the front of the stage. "When the music stops," he said, "the room will change from blue to anger." Charles nodded and continued to play. Karen and Nick looked at him. They continued for another minute, then stopped. The room exploded with accusations, as if the anger had been dying to get out. People confronted each other. Yusuf placed his hands over his ears and shook his head, turning away from anyone who came near him. Anthony pointed at others and laughed. Noticing him, Tonya stood alongside him and looked at where he was pointing. When Anthony laughed, she laughed, too. Sharon tried to run away from others, catching Anthony and Tonya's attention. They followed her, staying back just enough that she did not notice. Everyone appeared to be blaming someone else for something. After a minute or so, Ron pulled Elena, Donna, Terri, Yusuf, and Mona offstage, leaving Anthony, Chau, Denise, Sharon, and Tonya to continue the activity.

Beginning with Denise, the women circled Anthony and Tonya, pointing fingers at them and talking. Anthony moved backward in little circles, running into Chau, who pushed him toward the others. He was still in character. He was Pip, a New Yorker he created in a past writing activity. Pip is obnoxious and loud, a joker who exhibits a lot of movement and physical gestures but says little. Anthony tried to push his way out of the center of the group but was pushed back inside. Tonya turned on him, too. She stepped away from him and laughed heartily, then stepped toward him, waving her finger in his face. Anthony grimaced and turned away, faking a laugh once she was behind him. Sharon, who had been behind Tonya, turned away from her in the oppo-site direction from where Anthony was going. Chau and Denise stayed by Tonya's side, following Anthony across the stage. Finally, the women moved away, and as it appeared Anthony was free of them, Denise and Tonya con-fronted him again, slipping back in front of him. They bombarded him with a flurry of words. Anthony responded, yelling back and waving his hands in their faces as if to say "get out of here." When they didn't respond, he smiled and shrugged his shoulders, then walked away, waving his hand over his shoulder as he went, indicating to them to stay away. Reaching Sharon and Chau, who had moved across the stage, where they continued the movement by themselves, he tried to engage them in conversation. They acted like little girls, jumping around like frogs and giggling. Anthony imitated them, and Sharon rolled her eyes and turned away, pulling Chau with her.

Ron yelled for the music to become a part of what was going on, and the musicians began playing loudly. Denise and Tonya yelled over the sound, but I could not understand what they were saying. The sounds were harsh, a cacophony of noises of which the women were one part.

The others returned to the activity and the room changed from anger to indecision, then to white. "How does a white room make you feel?" Ron said. Finally the room became one of bending fingers, where the teenagers focused on each other's fingers. Sharon stood at center stage and held her hands in front of her. I was reminded of arthritic fingers. Yusuf recoiled from Sharon's gesturing. The teenagers stayed in character as they were thrust into each new scenario, adapting to where they were and responding to others.

When the activity was over, everyone met in a circle on the floor. Ron asked what they thought. Yusuf said he experienced things he had not before. His character was a man from his neighborhood who fronts as someone of great knowledge, but whom Yusuf saw as weak and unsure of himself, someone relying on others for reinforcement. His characterization of this man was of a person who heard voices in his head that mimicked the voice he used in interacting with others. Everyone was quiet, and I was not sure if Yusuf meant he knew more about his character now or that the movement was different than before.

Anthony said it took him a while "to lose himself," to get into the movement and then his character. Others agreed, insinuating that there is a process whereby your thinking changes and you actually feel comfortable doing the activity.

Later, Bryn used the movement and improvisation activities to define the writing activities. He had told me the year before that he looks for ways to tie writing in with the movement because he felt that a lot of what goes on in the movement activities—the imagery and emotions—is lost by the time the teenagers write. Over the course of the workshops, he tried such things as having teenagers write in the middle of movement and improvisation activities; turn to writing or moving whenever they wished; write immediately after an activity; and write in response to others' movement. Bryn's reasoning was pragmatic: The ensemble was creating a performance out of student writing, a performance that combined that writing with music, dance, and movement; thus, the best performance grew out of the interaction of these elements, all supporting one another.

This day, the image of the room—maybe as it was during the movement activity, maybe a room from one's past, or maybe as it was when they are writing—was the context for what was written. Bryn instructed the teenagers to imagine themselves going into a room and observing. "Get a sense of the room and compose a sentence in your mind that captures that sense, and then start writing." This sentence could be a snapshot of sorts, an image of an environment or context that one put one's character in, or another scenario, so to speak, that the teenagers will subsequently write about.

During the first part of the activity, the teenagers wrote about the room they were entering—what it looked like, what was in it, and how they felt. Sheila described the room she imagined like this:

Time, moving, and stillness . . . violence
Rums Swiss Almond Trolls
    that danced across the table
Honey marinated sperm
    that awakened his sleeping sex
Ransacking the house
    which held the clock set at midnight
Spotlights of lust
    and beds full of pain
Pulse barely moving
    and windows kidnapping rain
Cheddar cheese and buttered popcorn
Sourpatch kids and friendship bracelets
Kids begging for macaroni
And rats nibbling on old pieces of bologna
Old mops full of dust
and pissy underwear under the table
Four kids to a bed and roaches as pets
Three shards of families
And one dying generation
Twelve locks on the door
And three knives under your mattress
Twenty-four kids shot in drivebys
And two minds full of dreams.

She wrote this in about 15 minutes. The last two-thirds found its way into the script for that year's ensemble. It described a young woman torn between love and sexual desire, between a boyfriend pressuring her and what awaits her at home.

After describing the room, the teenagers paired up and shared their writing with each other. Sheila and Denise read theirs and talked about the imagery. They turned to the second part of the activity, taking what they had just written and finding a phrase in it that caught their attention, then writing a stream-of-consciousness piece that reflected how they felt in the room.

Denise, who had chased Anthony around the stage as if bent on confronting him, wrote for her second part:

> No one needs to come up to my face talking about revolution. I am a child of change, born of evolution, raised through hardship, surrounded by tall broken down struggles with busted windows and stairs that creak. When I cry I tell stories, each drop gives life to the oceans and puddles for others to drink from.
>
> My unimportance keeps the earth from falling off its axis and rolling down the alley to the gutter. Me and my ghetto keep the rest of the earth's assholes from suffering. We pay society's debt all on our own. No wonder we're always on food stamps—they owe us.

Significant here, I think, was not only the resemblance to Sheila's room, tweaked by Denise to capture her own perspective, but the similar evolution of Denise's piece to Sheila's, going from room description to individual concerns to community issues. Here also, Denise noted the significance of her stories as ways of both representing her community and keeping the world from going askew.

The power of written storytelling was something Denise was only starting to realize. Much of her early writing reflected an unwillingness to write. Her excuse was that she was a dancer and never wrote well before. In fact, during the first rehearsal of that year's ensemble, she wrote in a free write:

> Nothing Nothing It was like nothing likes ok but I don't wanna talk about it why cause cause cause why did I write that I feel really dumb just in case you thought I was a writer I'm not I'm a dreamer that's my profession this has nothing to do with shut up I'm a dreamer full time I go places you can't meet people you don't feel things unfelt because you're not courageous enough to step out of yourself and be a genuine person get rid of the fronts and let yourself shrink into sincerity that's what life's about?

Much of what shows up later in her writing, the poignant descriptions and succinct analysis of herself, her community, and how others see her, is hidden in this choppy rambling text about herself as a dreamer. She juxtaposes this with what she implicitly thinks a writer is. She rejects the ability of language to define who she is. Over time, Denise appeared to understand writing as a means of expressing who she is and not as something definitive of who she is not. As rehearsals went by, Denise became more adamant in writing about how she saw the world.

During the last part of the writing activity the teenagers described themselves alone in the room. Denise continued her reflections:

> I can't sleep 'cause I'm too tired. Can't cry 'cause I'm too sad. Quenching my thirst for culture by cramming tamales down my throat and bowing to the white Jesus with a mother named Guadalupe. I guess my only hope lies in men in coffins with hopes in their heads and names banished from history books, because not enough teachers knew how to roll their "R's". Salsa and stereotypes make my Mexicanness seem like a fad, a habit to grow out of, maybe even just a bad memory that a dangling pocket watch can fix.

Again, Denise addresses her own life and makes sense of how she is seen by others. Of the effect of the movement and improvisation activities on her writing, Denise later told me, as she pointed her index finger outward away from her eyes: "TeenStreet has not changed what's on that side of my eyes. It's changed what's behind them. It's changed the way I want to look at things. It's changed the way I want to see life."

After a short break, Ron put the teenagers into pairs. Each group created a short performance. This time, however, Ron told them to use minimal language and improvisation. They had 20 minutes to prepare. Yusuf and Donna created a scene about one of them being fooled by the other. Per Ron's instructions, they used minimal movement, but when they did move it was big and expressive. Elena and Denise created a scene about feelings of loss, using as few movements as possible. Charles and Terri created a hip-hop dance with a bass line that was behind the dance. Tonya and Chau created a dialogue with gestures and only three words. Karen was part of this group, too. She joined them during their performance, trying to interpret and retell the dialogue from afar with her own gestures. Anthony created a rap while Nick accompanied him by talking into his snare drum, which created a vibrating voice pattern. Sharon stood silently onstage as Sheila interpreted her minimal gestures by filling in the time between gestures with words. Every group performed at least twice. As each group performed, the rest of the ensemble was the audience.

They talked about the performances and what they saw. The performers told how they felt and what they wanted to convey. Ron, Anita, and the teenagers made suggestions, noting what worked well and what was confusing. Ron talked about the performers needing to be sure of what they wanted to convey and what they needed to do to convey it. For the teenagers, the focus was on telling how they felt in watching, or what the movement and improvisation conjured within them.

Using multiple ways of approaching a writing task and having others respond to what you wrote were common practices at TeenStreet, as was writing about the movement and improvisation activities. The language used to describe writing, although shrouded in expressions like *self-expression* and *emotional connection*, always wound back to communication of emotion to others. It was about defining one's world and one's place in it for others by ferreting out the experience behind the expression.

The focus placed on the body and experience while doing the movement and improvisation activities readied the teenagers to write from experience, both past and present. Ultimately, the teenagers relied on their understanding of the world as a source for meaning-making. The language that arose from the activities was expressive of experience and understanding. It was the voices of teenagers.

Because of one's unique perspective of the world and potentially unique voice, it is only through interaction that one's experiences can be more fully excavated and understood. Experiences become more meaningful in interaction, in our coming together to "hear" each of us "speak" of our experiences, even when language isn't a part of that dialogue. In interaction, voice is fully developed, given its communicative capacity in that we hear and see how others respond or address us and our existence, and, thus, are in a better position to make sense of our own and others' experiences.

6

Literacy Let Loose: Writing Instruction and the Honing of Voice

"Direct impact." When I first heard those words I thought of the crash dummies in the televised public service announcement for seat belt use. I saw white plastic mannequins—arms, legs, bodies, and heads wired together—propelled forward in a stripped-down version of an automobile. One body flies through the windshield as the front of the car crinkles and then, like a sponge, gives way to a wall. Pieces of metal and plastic fly about like water shaken loose. After a couple of seconds of slow-motion action, the car recoils and bounces backward, the damage done. One body, however, continues forward. The other, strapped in its seat belt, springs forward on impact, too, but bounces back, held tightly in its seat, no doubt the perfect position from which to watch the other catapult from the car. That was "direct impact" in all its ramifications, at least as it concerned seat belt use: A collision of dangerous proportions, with two responses, both having their own type of direct impact and repercussions.

The image had impact on me, reminding me of a line from *MadJoy*. In it, the narrator, recounting his mother's life lived in reverse, tells of his first love. She was "the seat belt that held my body to the earth," he says, wrapping his arms around himself as he stands on a darkened, empty stage. I had heard that line a hundred times, and there it was again, this time in my mind, fuller and more vivid than before.

Bryn said the words "direct impact" during a Saturday rehearsal in February of my second year. Before he arrived that day, the teenagers began an improvisation exercise where, from a standing position, they practiced falling and getting up. I was on the floor with them. Imagine a bunch of marionettes in the hands of unskilled puppet masters. Ron told us to take 10 seconds to reach the floor. Most of us were down by the time he counted from 10 to four. For the last four counts, we tossed our arms or legs around. From our sprawled positions, the exercise became one of reaching a standing position on the count of 10. We did it over and over, with little pause between efforts, until everyone was using the full 10 counts to reach the ground and get up in one motion. Then we did it in eight counts, sixes, fours, and twos, with bodies dropping like bricks. Arms flung downward to ease the impact, and knees buckled. Ten minutes of bouncing up and down left everyone out of breath.

We teamed up and did it all again, only this time we went up and down with partners without using hands. Bryn walked in as we started. He tossed his coat over the back of a chair and sat down. He pulled his journal from his bag. We struggled, backs pressed against each other, arms and shoulders trying to get leverage against the other's body. We wedged elbows or knees under our partners' arms or ribs to ease the journey downward or lift self and partner to a standing position. Bryn leaned forward. His open journal rested on his right knee, which crossed over the left leg. Before we finished, he bent over the journal, writing.

Ron counted the cadence and told people to be careful and support their partners. "Don't always go back-to-back," he said. "Try different ways." He jumped across the stage, took Anthony's place with Sharon, and showed us. Instead of being back-to-back, he and Sharon stood side-to-side. When they finished, Ron stepped away and Anthony returned. "You don't need to go down together," he said. "Experiment. Work with each other."

After 10 minutes, Ron turned to Bryn and nodded, and Bryn walked onstage, waving his hands to bring us together. We gathered in a circle, and Bryn said he wanted to talk about writing as it relates to falling. He wanted to talk about "direct impact." He hesitated, taking each of us in. "An important part of a story is its direct impact," he said momentarily, looking down at his journal. "Direct impact is something a writer controls." He asked what it is that makes a story good.

Donna said, "Rhythm," and someone else mumbled "plot," which was picked up by a couple of other teenagers.

"It has to be interesting," Anthony said. When everyone looked at him, he continued: "You know, actually mean something to you." His hands moved, adding emphasis to his words.

"Make you think about things," Elena added, just as Anthony was about to say something else. She stretched her legs in front of her and crossed them. Anthony nodded. She shrugged and smiled.

Terri, a junior in high school who, in her third year with TeenStreet, seemed younger than everyone else, mentioned Shakespeare and her belief that the meaning of his work does not always come to her immediately. It is something, she said, that "you have to think about for a while. Then it's like, *'OH yeah.'*"

No one else said anything. Bryn nodded and talked about how writers shape reality with the intent of drawing readers in by creating an alternative world with which they can associate.

It occurred to me months later, while reviewing my field notes and transcripts, that in this short discussion, Bryn and the teenagers were not talking about the same thing, although they were talking about an interaction of things. They were reflecting on aspects of communicating, its direct impact, and from where that impact comes. The movement exercise that morning dealt with communicating, with letting one's partner know where you are in relation to her lest you fall or move away, taking away needed and expected support. Bryn spoke of the writer's impact, or the ability to create or shape a reality that speaks to readers. The teenagers, maybe in response to Bryn, responded as readers, or addressees, noting the expectations (writing must have rhythm or plot) and responses (makes you think or seek out meaning) they bring to a text. The conversation centered around the reciprocal impact of writer, text, and reader.

Bryn told a story his sister had told him. A panhandler asked her for money, and each time she gave him some, he asked for more. The story ended with Bryn's sister frustrated and yelling at the panhandler. When she told him this story, Bryn said he believed it. Only later did he learn his sister had fabricated some of it. Bryn, in recounting his sister's duplicity, smiled and shook his head. He said he wanted to try something similar to what he had just done with his sister's story, and later, he wanted to try to do what his sister did with it. Bryn asked the teenagers to write a story someone else had told them. They spread out and went to work. When they finished, they gathered back in a circle and, one at a time, stood, and with eyes closed so they could not read what they wrote, retold their stories.

Many of the stories were extended jokes or anecdotes the teenagers had heard. For example, Elena wrote:

> This guy told about the time he went out. He had to stop and get some gas. After he got his gas he traveled on to the expressway. After a while

he decided he wanted a cigarette, so he lit one up. Then he noticed his arm was on fire (because somehow some gas leaked on his arm). He started speeding really bad then he got stopped by the police. When the policeman came to the car, he said, "You do know that you were going pretty fast?" He says, "Yes, but that was because my arm was on fire and I had to put my arm out the window to stop the fire." "Well," the cop said, "Okay, I excuse you from that so I won't give you a ticket for speeding, but I'm gonna have to give you a ticket for waving a firearm."

Others, however, were intricate tales of friends' experiences with evaluative comments added by the tellers. Some, like Denise's, recounted their own experiences and not a story someone else had told them. Denise wrote:

The only story I can think of is the embarrassing account of my reaction to a sneeze. Although saying "God bless you" may seem very normal— even muscle memory to most people, one incident of saying it in the wrong place has brought me much laughter even at the expense of people doubting my sanity. I dance with a youth troupe at a Buddhist cultural center. When I'm there I act like the biggest goof ball—but I really enjoy myself. As I was passing by one of the rooms a man came out who had probably just got through doing morning prayers when at the door he sneezed. Consciously I know saying "God bless you" is a Christian custom—but like I said it's muscle memory. So, loudly I said, "God bless you," as the man looked at me like I was crazy—and I got really upset not with myself for not thinking before I spoke but at him for not saying thank you.

When they finished, each teenager had two stories, the written one and the spoken one. They also had multivoiced (Bakhtin, 1986) stories, both the written and spoken retellings of something they had heard or experienced, the direct impact of each reverberating in the retellings, or as in the case of Denise and a few others, in the recallings. In a process probably not as linear as set out here, the teenagers had taken someone's experience as they experienced it vicariously, pulled it from their memories, written it down, and then retold it.

Later, after a movement exercise, the teenagers paired up and combined written stories, trying to incorporate the imagery and dialogue of both into one. Together, Denise and Elena wrote:

This guy told about the time he went out. He had to stop to get some gas. After he got his gas, he went on the expressway on his way to a Buddhist cultural center. He decided he wanted a cigarette, so he lit one up. Then he noticed his arm was on fire. He started speeding really fast and got stopped by the police. The policeman walked to the man's window and sneezed. The officer was Buddhist, and the man said, "God bless you." The officer didn't respond but said, "Are you aware that you were going really fast to be on an expressway?" The man said, "Yes but that was because my arm was on fire and I was trying to put the flames out." "Well," the cop said, "Okay, I'll excuse you for that but I'm gonna have to give you a ticket for waving a firearm." The man didn't get mad for the ticket, but he did get mad because the officer didn't say thank you for the sneeze.

Although their group effort incorporated much of what happened in both stories, it did not go beyond Elena's and Denise's individual efforts. Together, neither writer extended the other's story nor imaginatively remade and redefined it. The humor of both stories was absent from the group effort, and the combined story did not enthuse the other teenagers as much as the individual efforts did.

Interestingly, this was the only time during my two years at TeenStreet that Bryn asked teenagers to combine stories. During other group exercises, they shadowed others' writing, responded with a stream-of-consciousness piece, created an exquisite corpse, reflected and expanded on an image or phrase, or retold the story in another voice or from another perspective. What made this task difficult, I think, was the depersonalizing, or giving up, of voice involved in combining stories. Voices were diluted. Each teenager, in effect, objectified her voice to allow for the infusion of another's, which was also objectified. Instead of approaching the stories as objects to be interpreted, to be imbued with meaning, the teenagers combined stories image for image, with the final product controlled by what had already been said. I felt that Elena and Denise's interaction was contrived, the possibilities for exploration limited to what had already been said.

After the groups finished combining stories, each teenager took a turn performing his or her group's combined effort. The teenagers used the stories for both stage direction and dialogue. The performer's partner watched and wrote a stream-of-consciousness piece in response to the performance. Denise wrote this about Elena's performance:

cones wheat pinballs wind chimes primate confusion roam the countryside in search of a poetic saying metaphors for free pot brings creativity no light darkness comforts the lonely. 5, 10, 15, 20 I have a dime in my pocket. Rolling 'round with a tantrum on my mind. I fall wondering if this animal I see here will knock one out. I have two hearts of minds.

Here, Denise reflected in her own voice on Elena's performance. Her reflection, however, did not appear related to Elena's performance. She did not explicitly draw on any of the language, imagery, or plot of the story. She appeared to enter the story covertly. It was her voice speaking.

During the last part of the exercise, the teenagers used the original story, the combined story, and the stream-of-consciousness piece to write one last story. Denise wrote:

> This guy told me this story about how he went in search of two hearts. He started rolling around in a tantrum when he stopped for gas and hadn't found them. So he picked up his belongings and started to roam the countryside in my pocket. On the expressway, he saw a sign that said, "Free pot." That inspired him, so he picked some up and lit up. The joint lit up his arm and his hair and the darkness that comforted his loneliness. With his pain all ablaze, he turned to the left and with ka-mikaze creativity he slammed on the gas. I fell out of my mind on fire with primitive confusion falling on the ground passing right by the heart I was in search of. As I sneezed to put the fire out, the voice breathed his last breath as he said, "God bless you."

In this piece, direct impact came from every direction in a creative process that emphasized memory, interaction, observation, and relooking. The results were often absurd, a conglomeration of unrelated images such as a blind date's family that turns into rabbits right before her eyes or a child who relates being fathered by Big Bird. In Denise's case, the image of two people in search of something, maybe love ("two hearts"), maybe freedom ("roam the country-side"), or even, possibly, each other, evolved from someone telling Denise a story ("This guy told me this story . . . ") to Denise being a part of the story ("I fell out of my mind . . . "). The teller appears to be out of control, taking Denise on a destructive journey from drugs to speeding down the expressway. In the end, however, Denise is in control, her sneeze enough to quench the fiery blaze caused by pain. The "God bless you" phrase, a muscle reflex or cliché in her earlier writing, is recast as emblematic of Denise's survival and the teller's foreboding. The phrase is no longer trite or a cliché, but redefined as not quite a blessing but much more than politeness. Denise, who had ear-lier written about reflexively using the phrase and being embarrassed by it and then mad for not getting the usual response of "thank you," appropriated and transformed it to meet her own expressiveness. The stream-of-consciousness exercise appeared to trigger Denise's consciousness. She tapped into profound and personal feelings and thoughts, bypassing an overt understanding of "God bless you." She brought her voice to the fore, a voice that, although it recognized the phrase as a cliché, gave it a more significant and personal meaning.

The writing exercise this Saturday took a couple of hours to complete. Opinions, interpretations, and beliefs that formed over time—from the first hearing of a friend's story, and even before, from how story is understood—came to the fore in a process Aristotle called rhetoric's purpose. Interpretations, probable truths, and beliefs propelled the writer on. Aristotle's understanding of rhetoric, described by Erika Lindemann (1995) as a "form of reasoning about probabilities, based on assumptions people share as members of a community" (p. 42), resonates with Bryn's notion of what a writer does to impact readers. In this writing exercise, the give-and-take of the language use among participants, across sign systems—oral and written—and within individuals was dialogical. It was enlivened in interaction and emboldened through inquiry and sharing—that is, oral, written, and physical interaction—while being grounded in the participants' lives. Direct impact, in this sense, flowed not only through imaginal interaction among participants but also through experiences and reflections on experiences. Although one's voice—one's stories—can have direct impact on others, it is through one's own experience and reflection on experience that one impacts the self, that one self-reflects and comes to have a voice. Others' stories are meaningful when allowed to speak to whom we are and when we speak of them with our own voices.

Socrates called such voice, or language use, "living speech." He, however, was referring to oral language. I include writing because in speaking of language and its dialogicality, I see the written word entwined with oral language, nurturing it and being nurtured by it. A child's oral language use influences how she talks about text. In her interaction with others about text, the child's understanding of written language also is shaped. During these interactions, the child's conceptions of what written language is and what it does are formed.

In this chapter, I bring my discussion of TeenStreet's creative process back to writing, particularly what I think writing does for the teenage participants. Oral language is invariably part of my beliefs about written language, just as it is part of learning to write, both as its prerequisite and its companion. I also take a selective look at precedents of writing research and theory that buoy what I presented in previous chapters. The research and theory are limited to what figures in my analysis of the writing instruction at TeenStreet. Much research and theory, such as that of Donald Graves, Peter Elbow, and writing process and whole language proponents, are not presented here because these views are set out clearly in other texts and usually address school-based contexts. I end this chapter by formulating a theory of listening—an ideology, really—that fosters voice development arrived at through experience at TeenStreet.

SOME PARAMETERS: A SELECTIVE HISTORY

Throughout history, composition research has involved ferreting out processes and instructional modes that have direct impact on student writing. The history of writing instruction in Western societies can be linked to the longer history of rhetoric and the classical rhetorical traditions of Ancient Greece. The history of rhetoric has tried to emulate the master rhetors of Ancient Greece by teaching students models of persuasion or by imparting tactical strategies. These models and strategies were designed for oral discourse. Many of them, however, influence writing instruction today.

A Framework: Aristotle and Plato

The one constant in the history of rhetorical practice, from oral to written discourses, is rhetoric's goal of inducing others to cooperate or agree in one way or another with the rhetor (Lindemann, 1995). Lost in this goal for many years was the Aristotelian notion of rhetoric as a practical art and a way of knowing. Rhetoric, according to Aristotle, helps humans arrive at who they are, uncovering potential or possibilities in a quest for actuality. Aristotle believed that rhetoric is our prime means of creating common or shared knowledge (Corbett, 1990).

The dichotomy between the Aristotelian notion of rhetoric as community-builder and other classical rhetors' notions, notably Plato's form or Truth, has fueled the paradigms of writing research and instruction for the last 2,500 years. On the one side, Plato conceived of form as a distinct entity—the Ideal—separate and independent of matter and, in the case of creativity, something to be emulated. On the other side, although he conceived of form similarly to Plato, Aristotle postulated that the Ideal or form exists in matter and that matter, through constant and dynamic change and exchange, is capable of reaching the Ideal, if not in total at least in part. Rhetoric is subject to give-and-take, not absolute truth.

Platonic form, or formalism, and its influence on writing instruction have dominated the teaching of composition. Formalist instruction through the ages has always tried to impart some type of truth to its learners, whether it is with subject matter or rhetorical form. Those who appeared incapable of learning the truth were often excluded from those Discourses that dominated specific structures of society, such as professional, academic, and government Discourses. Upholders of these Platonic notions and Discourses often equate language with power (Tompkins, 1980), with the intention of controlling the flow of power by controlling or defining how language should be used. Literacy was and still is often presented as a known entity that only those who meet established criteria have access to (Cook-Gumperz, 1986). This is literacy as adaptation and state of grace. Aristotelian notions of literacy and language use, however, are more yielding. That is, writing instruction is premised on human potential or how one can use literacy to define one's life.

The history of composition instruction and literacy learning suggests a concept of literacy that breaks down along Platonism or formalism and Aristotelian and, at times, dialogical lines. Although a dichotomy is simplistic, this brief historical summary establishes a context that heightens the significance of the TeenStreet creative process in light of past views and current understandings of literacy theory and composition research, and in light of the emphasis placed on formalist instruction, including standardization, by recent educational reform initiatives.

Oral Language and the Search for Meaning

Even with the fracturing of the Platonist–Aristotelian dichotomy in literacy research over the last 30 years, instructional practices seldom address or draw on students' oral language ability, particularly when that ability doesn't jibe with mainstream or "standard" English. Nor do instructional practices give much thought to language's relationship to physicality and consciousness. Instruction is still often adversarial to students' oral language, conceived as a way to "correct" speaking and writing skills. This deficit educational model— meaning the students are assumed to be lacking in skills or ability—is premised on the need to impart those skills and abilities and thus often misses what students know and experience.

Although most formalists, following Noam Chomsky's (1957) lead, consider speaking ability to be innate, others, among them sociolinguists, associate learning to speak as a part of our socialization into human activity that begins at birth (Bruner, 1983). We aren't taught to speak so much as we come to acquire language through lived experience. Simple observations of children show that without direct instruction in grammar they become competent oral language users, usually by the age of four. That the grammar children develop in learning to speak is affected by experience, including literacy events, is evidenced in children's growing awareness of patterns of language and the adjustments they make in language use. For example, it is not uncommon for a child, once she realizes that -ed is a common past tense marker, to overgeneralize and begin adding -ed to all verbs, including irregular ones she had previously formed correctly.

Some theorists and researchers (Halliday, 1987; Snow, 1983) believe that conscious reflection on grammar rules inhibits speaking and writing efforts. The patterns of language, including syntactical patterns, become more evident with relevant and meaningful speaking, reading, writing, and listening opportunities. Such patterning, I theorize, is a continuation of the process of learning oral language in that we are always honing and revising our language practices. I also suggest that although oral language development and literacy development are two distinct continuums in language development, they depend on one another for continued development beyond the mastery of a primary Discourse. Thus, our experience with and use of text influences our language use and vice versa.

Miriam Camitta (1993), in her study of Philadelphia high school students' vernacular writing, provides an example of language patterning. She recognized teenagers' practice of appropriating words and phrases from oral traditions, popular culture, and written texts for their own texts. The students reinvented the texts by recontextualizing them in their own writing, by making them their own. Camitta calls this practice patchwork composing, a practice effused with Bakhtinian (1986) ideas of multivoicedness, ventriloquating, and heteroglossia. These ideas suggest that our voices are filled with the voices of others even as we say that which is particular to us.

Although researchers have focused on the semantic aspects of patterning or patchwork composing, the syntactical aspects that are appropriated are often the most recognizable features of these texts. They are also features closely related to oral language use. The negative focus given these features in formalist instruction often drives a wedge between oral and written language. For example, Lu's (1994) description of her basic writers class's effort to understand a classmate's use of "can able to" exemplifies what Hartwell (1985) calls the grammar of the head. Lu's student's use of "can able to" made sense to her and the other students after the class discussed it. The phrase followed a logical, syntactical pattern that the student had arrived at through her experiences of learning English. It conveyed the student's understanding of the world. The grammar of the head, Hartwell writes, is an "eminently usable knowledge—the way we make our life through language—but it is not accessible knowledge; in a profound sense we do not know we have it" (p. 111). We arrive at it in the living of life and in our interactions with others. We look for ways to convey meaning in particular contexts, and in doing so, we are drawn to how meaning is conveyed by others. This is how we make meaning of the world.

"WHO YA SMACKIN'?": PROJECTING ONE'S VOICE IN THE WORLD

At TeenStreet, meaning-making arises from an intense focus on one's body in time and space through visual imagery. It proceeds in the "coming forth" of one's voice from one's body in ways described in the previous chapter, including somatic and mental image-making and reflection. This coming forth is often the subject matter for writing and is bound up in voice or orality. In the previous chapter, I described the evolution of mental and somatic imagery to interaction and writing. Here I want to focus on Ron, Anita, and David's efforts to make the teenagers conscious of their and others' voices as they arise from a focus on imagery.

Although voice exercises came to play a greater role in the movement and improvisational exercises over time, discussions about voice began during the first rehearsal of each year's ensemble. Ron and Anita talked about voice as a physical embodiment, and the need for the teenagers to focus on that place within the body from which it arises. Many of the exercises involved listening to sounds coming from one's own body and from the bodies of others. In December of both years that I was a participant-observer, David Schein introduced voice exercises that focused on verbal interaction and the shaping of one's voice in response to others'. In subsequent rehearsals, Ron and Anita incorporated these exercises into the movement, with dialogue becoming more prominent in all the exercises.

During the first rehearsal of both years I was there, Ron responded to teenagers' yawns during warm-ups by saying, "If you yawn, make it a really big yawn." He gave them an example of what he meant and introduced an imperative that resounded during all rehearsals: "Make yourself be heard." In November of my first year, after a writing exercise, the teenagers gathered in a circle to read what they wrote. Ron told them to read as if their mouths were loose and the shaping of a sound required a full extension of the mouth and tongue, an exaggeration of the normal tongue placement and mouth movement. He told them to play with the sounds of the words. "Engage the language," he said. "Open your mouth a lot."

Bonnie read first. After 10 seconds, Ron moved opposite her to the other side of the circle. "Hit me with your words," he said, interrupting her. "Send them out and smack me with your words."

Bonnie leaned forward and read louder, her voice rising and falling in pitch and rhythm.

After Bonnie finished, Mona began reading. Ron interrupted her asking "Who are you talking to?"

"You," she said, in midsentence.

"Good. Smack me with your words. You got a big, wonderful mouth. Use it," Ron said.

Mona hesitated and smiled lightly. She looked down at her paper. When she looked up and spoke, her voice was filled with expression.

Ron asked each teenager who she was smacking. After each named another person—usually the one across from her—he said, "Smack them with your words. Send them across. They should make a mark on the forehead when you're done." He also said repeatedly: "Say it like you're doing it."

From these moments of projecting voice, the teenagers explored during warm-ups where their voices come from as a lead into voice exercises. The backdrop for these exercises was Ron's admonition to be nonjudgmental. Four weeks before the "Who ya smackin'?" scene just described, the teenagers stood in a circle at center stage. Ron told them to begin talking, saying whatever came to mind by listening to what others were saying. Within a minute, everyone was talking at the same time. After a few minutes, Ron yelled for Donna to continue talking and everyone else to stop.

Donna's voice slowed and dropped in volume for a moment as her eyes moved around the circle. "Don't stop," Ron said. Donna glanced at him. Her voice rose. She told of her efforts to get to rehearsal on time and waiting for the train and being late and hating to be late because Ron always asks why she is late. She never has an excuse he accepts, and she is mad because she knows she tried to get here on time. Everyone's eyes were on her. Donna looked around, speaking to everyone. After a few minutes, Ron told the rest of the teenagers to start talking again, and about half of them were talking about their trips to rehearsal that morning.

Other exercises were similar in that the teenagers kept talking and didn't worry about what they said. Often these "free-for-all" speech events or stream-of-consciousness voice exercises were preceded during warm-ups and small mind exercises by a focused exploration of different sounds a voice can make. A week before the exercise described above, after the warm-ups, with everyone still on the floor, Ron told them to begin the wave exercise by massaging their butts and backs into the floor. He told them to begin humming so that only those closest could hear. A low, stereophonic hum engulfed the room.

Ron instructed the teenagers to momentarily put their hands on their heads. "Change the pitch of your hum and then feel the vibration, how it changes, too," he said. "Hold your other hand on your stomach and feel the air go in and out." The teenagers continued moving, the imaginary waves rolling them onto their stomach and knees. Ron motioned for them to start moving closer together. Everyone crawled slowly toward the center of the circle until they were side by side, their heads touching each other.

"Can you feel the vibration of each other?" Ron asked. "Put your hand in front of your face and feel the air coming out." Donna, after feeling her own breath, put her hand in front of Jared's mouth. Ron called for the humming sound to change to a continuous long e sound.

The sounds evolved from long e to long u, to long o, to short a. After five minutes, Ron said, "Loosen up the mouth and lips and repeat, 'The breath is the voice, the voice is the breath.'" Everyone stumbled through it the first time, and Ron repeated it. After a couple of tries, the teenagers spoke the line in unison. "Increase the air output but don't raise the volume," Ron said. "Repeat, 'The lips pop the pees, the tongue taps the tees.'" Everyone began, many of them having trouble remembering what to say at first and stopping to listen. Finally, after about 30 seconds, everyone was together. "Spit if you have to," Ron said. "Look across at the person in front of you. If they're not doing anything, you have to wonder why they're here. Focus on someone. Keep repeating it." As everyone continued, Ron listened and spoke over them every once in a while, saying: "It's like the words are fish in your mouth. Let them swim around in there." "Practice saying stuff fast. It will be understandable." "Play with the pitch." "Loosen up the tension in your mouth." "Look at the person across from you."

Later, the teenagers paired up. Facing each other, partners began talking to one another nonstop, saying whatever came to mind. Ron called out a name and everyone but that person stopped talking. Everyone took a solo for about 30 seconds.

These voice exercises focused on the physicality of voice and the extent to which physical exertion influences voices. The exercises introduced the teenagers to the idea that voice represents one's physical presence. What was said was of secondary importance to being able to speak about how one felt and how one wanted to convey those feelings. Although interaction was part of the exercises, the communicative aspect of interaction was less important than the teenagers' growing awareness of how to use voice as a way of impacting others and how others' voices impact their own. The voice and its effect on others were described by Ron in physical or bodily terms, as if one is doing something physical when speaking and that doing physically affects others. Voice is not only a creation of the body but also a communicative ability that rests on how it impacts others' bodies.

Ron, Anita, David, and Bryn introduced voice to the teenagers as something arising from the body, as something contingent on experience, on interpreting experience, including their own and others'. Voice was cast as more than expression: voice is one's response to the world. The voice answers others', reflects others', and is effused with others' voices, but it is one's own voice arising from one's own body. Voice is the speaking consciousness, a conglomeration of overt and covert consciousnesses, public and private extrapolations. It includes the speaking person's "perspective, conceptual horizon, intention, and world view" (Wertsch, 1991, p. 51). It exists, always, in a social context, shaped in interaction, even as it is one's own.

OTHERS' VOICES IN THE SHAPING OF ONE'S OWN VOICE

As warm-ups evolved into movement exercises, we focused on the type of sounds we were making as we moved. We changed the pitch and rhythm of our voices, creating nonsense words. After the movement exercise, we focused exclusively on voice. In groups of twos, with one person leading, the other tried to say the same words at the same time as her partner was speaking. Face to face, with only a foot or so between partners, the person doing the following had to attend to not only what was said but how it was said, where the words were coming from and leading to. Partners had to anticipate what was coming next by focusing on what was said, by figuratively trying to step into the other's time and place. Roles were reversed until the exercise evolved to where there was no leader, each partner trying on the other's words even as he prepared to say something himself. The exercise required a connected-ness where one was consumed by the sounds of the other. One had to learn to give and take, both to lead and follow, based not only on what was said but on how it was said and how one's partner looked.

David spoke of the process eventually evolving to where one breaks the rules of the exercise, able to enter a true dialogue premised on listening to what is said. This breaking of rules enabled one to step vicariously into the time and place of the speaker and then back into one's own time and space to respond. One's own voice accounted for the other's voice, what the other said and might say. The exercise was not unlike exercises used by classical rhetors that emphasized *prosopopoeia*, or speaking for an imaginary or absent character. Indeed, TeenStreet movement, improvisation, voice, and writing exercises were often followed by character development exercises that re-quired creating another's perspective. In speaking to the theory behind the classical rhetor's use of prosopopoeia, Corbett (1990) wrote:

> Being asked to put yourself in the shoes of someone else forces you to imagine what that someone else is like. You have to assume a consciousness, a disposition, an attitude other than your own. . . . What all this ultimately comes to is a growing awareness of the I-Thou relationship that is so vital for success in the workaday world. (p. 201)

Although what is said and done during the TeenStreet exercises arises from the teenagers' perspectives, others' influence on the words and actions is sig-nificant. Having a voice that communicates is precipitated by listening and making sense of one's time and place in the world in relation to others', which means making sense of another's time and place. Bryn drove this point home during a rehearsal the next week. After a shower exercise, he asked the teen-agers how they would relate the movement exercises to hearing.

Yusuf said we often take our hearing for granted. We automatically as-sume we know what it is we have heard. We cannot do that in the movement, however. We have to always be attentive and watching others.

Bryn pointed out that the movement exercises involved hearing in that we have a dialogue going on in our heads while moving. There is also, how-ever, the concept of mis-hearing, "which opens up a whole new world to you."

Without explaining what he meant, Bryn said he wanted to read a list of phrases to the teenagers. He asked them to write down what they heard. "I'll only read each one once," he said, "so listen and write what you hear."

He began, saying, "Notice bright wick."

"What?" Anthony said, followed by the same query from Denise and Mona.

Bryn shook his head and did not say anything. Instead, he waited a few seconds and then read the second phrase: "Hilarious desk-mounted clown."

Mona looked up, her mouth tightly closed, forming a thin line. Bryn smiled at her, and she bent over her notebook and started writing.

"Move with the words," Bryn said softly. "Try to feel the words as they're said. Listen with your whole body."

He continued: "Clasp your shadow to the ground."

After 25 more phrases, Bryn told them to listen with a character's ears. "How would that character hear these phrases?" Bryn asked.

After about half a minute, he began again. "In any event, the history of all is not the history of each."

"Ah, man, that's too long," Yusuf said, looking up and laughing.

"Did you hear it?" Bryn asked.

"Yeah."

"Okay." Bryn waited a few moments, then said, "Sweating in a crouch."

After another 25 phrases, Bryn asked how switching over to a character affected hearing.

"I played around with the character's hearing," said Sharon.

"Yeah, maybe I was tired, but I didn't try to listen as closely as we went on," Yusuf said.

Charles smiled. "After a while, you play with it. Imagine what you hear."

"You were reading too fast, so I didn't get them all," Mona said, shaking her head.

Donna said she focused on the ones she liked. "Some of them sounded nice. Those were the ones I got."

They talked about the difference between listening to themselves and others listening to them. Yusuf said, "I would imagine it is hard for others who are not familiar with us to really listen and understand."

Others agreed, with Denise noting that in many cases most people do not listen even when they say they are.

"They hear, but they don't know what you mean," Sheila added.

"Or they don't care," Donna said. She shrugged. "Sometimes I don't care."

"How you say it is important," Bryn noted.

As a segue to writing and the importance of voice in one's writing, Bryn noted that we need to sensitize ourselves to what we are writing. He spoke of getting into the words and sentences and unearthing the meaning, of getting behind the words. "It's a way of listening, to really get into the words and find their meaning. Rewriting," he said, "is like listening to yourself. It's as much a furrowing for meaning as it is a weeding out of the excess." The notion of pushing at the boundaries of one's life, something Ron stressed in the movement and improvisation, seemed relevant here, too. Bryn suggested that we push further into the thoughts that lead to the words in order to understand what others as speakers and we as writers mean. This was something Bryn talked about with each teenager, often asking them to pick a phrase from their own writing and "get into it," dig deep into the phrase and the meaning behind it. Such pushing and digging were instigated and supported by imaginal interaction, where teenagers interacted with each other and explored their understanding and experiences using multiple means of communicating.

Bryn talked of listening closely as a way of developing voice. Denise's last revision of her story took on multiple voices, which she had heard and read, to become uniquely her own voice. I see this process of listening and bringing together multiple voices as the quintessential aspect of voice development and writing instruction. It is process that gives writing lasting relevance in all contexts. It can potentially transform contexts or Discourses, while helping us to both make sense of and redefine contexts. On a larger scale, it helps us define ourselves in relation to others, including our own physicality and perspective. How we listen to others also greatly affects our ability to create activities or environments that perpetuate such listening. Indeed, it is how we listen to others, how we interact and define ourselves in relation to others, that ensures the life of a story and the possibilities that writing can afford us.

MAKING SENSE OF THE WORLD

Imagine the implications of a perspective of writing instruction that posits oral and written language as sources for fuller understanding of language use and one's own perspective and understanding of the world. If language is a mediational tool with which we make sense of the world and communicate, the importance of written language as a tool for furthering our understanding of language and as a source of human agency and empowerment is evident. Implications of this perspective include: 1) If one controls another's use of language, that is, if one controls another's way of naming the world, including how it relates to literacy, one has influence over the other's conception of the world; and 2) if one is encouraged not only to reflect on the oral and written language of others but also to use oral and written language to explore one's own understanding, one's use of language, both semantically and syntactically, and thus communicatively, is enhanced, as is others'.

Oral and written language use not only hone literacy skills, they also make one aware of the patterns of language that go unrecognized when learning to speak. In reading and writing, we see the patterns of English. We unlock the communicative mystery of language. Formalists might agree with this notion of seeing patterns and say that this is what grammar instruction does, but with a greater focus on patterns. This response, however, misses the point of how people use language. The patterns must be encountered in meaningful contexts and have communicative value, similar to the process by which we learn to speak. Our lives are the key to unlocking that communicative mystery, beginning with learning language as an infant. Thus, literacy is a social practice reflective of both a particular context and a person's place in that context. Literacy educators should strive to make this evident to students. This belief guides my theorizing and understanding of literacy and human relations in the rest of this chapter.

PREWRITING REDEFINED

James Moffett (1968) noted that "The stuff to be conceived and verbalized [in language use and writing instruction] is primarily the raw stuff of life, not language matters themselves. Rendering experience into words is the real business of school" (p. 114). Like Moffett, James Britton and others also saw language as a way of representing experience. However, Britton saw the relationship as reciprocal: language influences experience, also. His attack on formalist teaching methods was the most ardent of the time. He noted that "dummy run" exercises that had students writing according to prescribed forms, such as the five-paragraph essay, not only ignored a student's experiential knowledge but, in effect, made that knowledge invisible to the student, thus affecting future experience.

In 1971, Janet Emig offered her own critique of formalism and stated that teachers should be concerned with the writing processes of students. She pointed out that writing is a recursive process nurtured in a writer's reflection on experience, with such reflection often coming at the beginning stages of writing, or during prewriting.

Emig (1971) defined prewriting as

> that part of the composing process that extends from the time a writer begins to perceive selectively certain features of his inner and/or outer environment with a view to writing about them—usually at the instigation of a stimulus—to the time when he first puts words or phrases on paper elucidating that perception. (p. 39)

Prewriting is the way a writer approaches the writing task and the accumulation of information—understanding, knowledge, and experience—he brings to it. I suggest that everything TeenStreet does outside of writing, including the movement, voice, improvisation and music activities, is prewriting.

My initial impressions of TeenStreet were of a program designed to help teenagers tap into their own experiences in order to foster writing development. Prewriting was at the center of these efforts. Of course, initial impressions are usually simplistic. Yet the movement and improvisation exercises described in previous chapters, although not defined as such, are prewriting strategies that, in effect, do what many composition scholars and researchers believed prewriting exercises should do—they help students tap into their experiences.

Concerning prewriting strategies, Hayes and Flower (1980b) distinguished between procedural plans and content-specific plans for generating ideas. Procedural plans are usually sequential note-taking or outlining techniques that keep writers on track as they write. Such plans are best suited for students comfortable or at home in the classroom writing context and thus able to translate something as specific yet minimal as a list or outline into a fleshed-out piece of writing. At TeenStreet, such plans helped fill in gaps in scripts or fine-tune specific scenes by playing around with the language of the script. It was during these times that the nature of project-based curriculum or goals was most evident, because the teenagers knew what the result was to be and were more or less fine-tuning what was already there, working more on presentation than content.

Content-specific plans reference what the writer knows. Important to these plans is the writer's ability to find a focus, which Hayes and Flower noted was seldom done successfully by the novice writers they observed. Finding a focus appears contingent on context and students' abilities to function or feel comfortable within that context. Focusing is an idiosyncratic endeavor, which may explain, in part, why so many writers have difficulty doing it, particularly within highly structured contexts with which they are not familiar and in which their language practices are seen as inferior.

Hayes and Flower also identified organizing and goal-setting, or establishing criteria by which to judge text, as important aspects of prewriting. They noted that criteria do not need to be clearly defined for a writer to be successful, but that the writer does need to have a sense of what he wants to accomplish, which is the quintessential element of project-based curriculum. It is easy to see the connection between determining criteria and having a purpose for writing. Successful writers have reasons for writing and interests in accomplishing something even if it is not necessarily clear at the start. Thus, in preparing to write a person needs to have an idea, or maybe ideas, of what he wants to do, how he wants to go about doing it, and what the product will possibly look like.

Two aspects of language, however, stand out as possible reasons for a correlation between prewriting and length and craftsmanship of a piece of writing. One, as Hillocks (1986) hypothesizes, is that "[w]hen children learn that the requirements of written prose are different from conversation, they activate more extensive memory searches" (p. 33). Children learn to make this distinction over time through oral readings of written text, often done as story-book reading by parents or teachers. For students from oral-language-domi-nant backgrounds or whose literacy experiences are not similar to those of the classroom, the distinction may not be well formulated, readily apparent, or even much of a distinction. Thus, prewriting activities may be critical in mov-ing students from an oral language or other different literacy orientation to being prepared to write communicatively and meaningfully even as oral lan-guage plays a significant part in writing instruction. At TeenStreet, this transi-tion is described as getting teenagers to experiment or see things differently, making prewriting exercises focusing devices, designed for teenagers to hone in on their own and others' experiences. Oral language, or discussion, is often part of this focusing.

The second aspect of language that foreshadows the correlation between prewriting and the issues of length and craftmanship has to do with language's relationship to consciousness and meaning-making. Pianko (1979) noted that "writing should begin with an idea developing out of students' confrontation with life" (pp. 17–18). Prewriting, thus, is the bringing to bear on the task what the writer knows, and extending that knowledge through inquiry. A large part of inquiry is observation and exploration, two purposes for the movement and improvisation exercises at TeenStreet. Meaning-making depends on mem-ory recall, and it is this that prewriting tries to initiate.

Britton (1993) posits that writing fluency, in a reciprocal fashion, leads to greater memory recall. Yet the same probably could be said about any interac-tive process, requiring the participants to reflect on what is said, read, written, seen, heard, or felt. The purpose of memory recall is to help one plan and organize the writing task. Thus, it is reasonable to conclude, as Hayes and Flower do (1980a), that one way to improve writing is to improve the planning process that is part of it. Memory recall, however, is tied to experience and covert consciousness, to tapping into what the writer knows. Memory recall, if it is really memory recall and not a cursory reflection on what a person knows about a topic or theme, is grounded in the writer's memory, which moves beyond the topic or theme to encompass the life of the writer, with the theme or topic addressed from the writer's perspective.

Bereiter and Scardamalia (1982) concluded that children learning to write must also learn to access information from their memories. My own classroom teaching experience, similar, I believe, to many teachers' experi-ences, confirms the difficulty of getting students to reflect on what they really know. Formalist notions of composition, which most students experience at some time in their education, have taught many students not to place much credence in what they know or in the experiences they bring to school. Also, many of the strategies used in schools to access memory are procedural, drawing on knowledge as a guide or outline and not involving students in any type of exploration or assessment of memory. Few strategies actually revive memory or bring memory to life or require students to express information garnered from memory. In this regard, in my earliest field notes, I recognized what was happening at TeenStreet as distinct from anything I had seen before in a writing instruction environment.

Discussing a topic is probably the most common prewriting strategy for tapping into memory. Yet discussions seldom extend beyond 10 or 15 minutes in most classrooms and usually leave a student with only a few phrasal notes. Dramatization and improvisation are two strategies that have been successful in the early grades (Dyson, 1989; Paley, 1981, 1990; Wolf, 1994, 1996), particularly in helping students re-look at writing or see it as performative. At Teen-Street, these and other strategies were woven together, and with the emphasis on focus, criteria, and goals, they worked well not only in getting teenagers to write but also to reconceptualize what writing means to them. Imaginal interaction allowed teenagers to access memory and imagination and learn from others' memories and imaginations in ways that suggest that writing is an expressive mediational tool. Indeed, writing became the artifact of excavated memories, both real and imagined.

In building a writing curriculum, coming up with strategies that invite students to reflect on their experiences and what they want to say about those experiences is vital. Although these may be considered prewriting activities, they are activities that should be incorporated into all phases of writing. As a recursive process, writing demands constant reflection and focus on what is happening and what needs to happen.

I posit the honing of meaning-making and communicative capabilities as a matter of developing voice. Voice is the expression of one's perspective from one's own place and time. However, perspective-taking, at its fullest, recognizes the heteroglossia of voices in the world—or, as Ron says, uses the "big mind" and takes in everything that is around the actor. Perspective-taking is the melding of covert and overt consciousness in an effort to see the world as fully as possible without relegating one's own perspective—one's own bodily position—to anything less than the anchor from which one acts. Donna's discussions about time in Chapter 4 are examples of this melding. She spoke of different contexts and people from a self-conceptualized perspective, verbalizing who she is in relation to others in those contexts. Voice is an action, a verbal response to the world, and a product of a person's existence in the world. Writing is but one means of expressing voice. In imaginal interaction, voice is defined and bolstered by other representational means, such as somatic and mental imagery.

Prewriting at TeenStreet is everything but the actual writing, because everything is geared toward expression, of which writing is but one means. Activities are designed to bring forth narrative formation or teenagers' stories for all to hear and interpret. Not only do teenagers work at defining their voices but, through imaginal interaction, they also work at making them accessible to others. Voice development was contingent on listening and making sense of others' voices. Many of these activities, like the movement and improvisation activities described in previous chapters, were prewriting activities that not only prepared teenagers for writing but also helped them reconceptualize what writing can do for them.

The interaction of teenagers' voices and bodies presented in this and the previous chapters is premised on participants' need to listen closely to others in order to hone their own voices. This interaction is grounded in the theory of dialogism that grew out of M. M. Bakhtin's theory (1990, 1993). I want to burnish that theory to make explicit how we might listen to others and how this way of listening fosters meaningful literacy use and development.

MULTIPLE VOICES, MULTIPLE VIEWS OF THE WORLD

Concerning human interaction, M. M. Bakhtin (1990, 1993) wrote of aesthetic contemplation as the act of "empathizing into an individual object of seeing—seeing it from inside in its own essence" (1993, p. 14). Voice activities that had teenagers "standing in the place" of others or anticipating what others would say fostered this empathy. Bakhtin wrote that the "first step in aesthetic activity is my projecting myself in him [or her] and experiencing his [or her] life from within him [or her]. I must experience—come to see and to know—what *he [or she]* experiences; I must put myself in his [or her] place and coincide with him [or her], as it were" (1990, p. 25). Yet this contemplative act is never fully empathetic, simply because of the perspective from which I see. Because the other already occupies a particular place and time, that is, because she has her own unique perspective, and because my empathizing is grounded in my own time and place, I never really know another's experience. We each have unique perspectives on the world and never can fully know each other's.

Bakhtin's (1993) conception of aesthetic empathy focuses on the speaker and what the speaker gains from her interactions with others. As such, his concern appears to be with maintaining the integrity of the speaker. He wrote:

> I empathize *actively* into an individuality and, consequently, I do not lose myself completely, not my unique place outside it, even for a moment. It is not the object [what another person says] that unexpectedly takes possession of me as the passive one. It is *I* who empathize actively into the object: empathizing is *my*

act, and only that constitutes its productiveness and newness. . . . Empathizing actualizes something that did not exist either in the object of empathizing or in myself prior to the act of empathizing, and through this actualized something Being-in-event [one's lived life] is enriched (that is, it does not remain equal to itself). (p. 15)

Empathizing is tinted with our understanding or with the multiple voices that make up our understanding, thus transforming not only ourselves but also that which we see and hear, offering up possibilities that can define our own lives and the lives of others.

TeenStreet worked at this idea of losing oneself completely in another person as a way of pushing at the boundaries of understanding and expressing openly what is normally not voiced. The fact that open expression was often reached and then lost shows how difficult this type of empathizing is. For example, one activity, called Zen Radio, had groups of three or four get up and start riffing off each other, just talking back and forth and following each other. During a rehearsal in December of my first year, after a voice activity similar to the one described earlier in this chapter where the teenagers stood face to face and tried to anticipate what each other would say, David pulled all but one of the groups—Anita the Assistant Director, Jared, and Lisa—off the floor. He told the other teenagers to get notebooks. Two teenagers were to write everything that was said by Anita, Jared, and Lisa, that is, everything they could get down. The others were to write whatever they wanted, focusing either on what the group was saying or what they, as writers, were thinking. David told Anita, Jared, and Lisa to start talking, focusing on and responding to each other's words.

Anita stood between Jared and Lisa. As they talked, one of them mentioned the color brown, and Anita started talking about brown milk and chocolate milk with white marshmallows.

Jared interrupted her. "What are you talking about?" he said. "Do you know what brown is?" He started talking about other colors—red, blue, green—finally saying that red dirt was really brown. Then he said that his skin is brown. "Brown skin," he said over and over, "like the soil, like the earth." Jared continued, talking about the African-American labor experience as workers of the soil and assembly lines.

Lisa looked at him and then held her arm up to his. Anita was still between them. Their arms were aligned in front of her. "My skin is light brown," Lisa said.

Anita stared down at their arms, and looked at Lisa first and then Jared. She held up her arm next to theirs. Hers was a pale red color, not quite pink but not white either. "I'm a marshmallow," she said.

"Chocolate with marshmallow middle," Lisa said, laughing. "Ooh, I like chocolate with marshmallow middles. They taste good."

Anita concurred, and talked about the chocolate melting on her face and the gooey marshmallow getting stuck between her teeth.

Jared would not let Lisa and Anita steer the conversation away from his concerns. He pulled his arm away and rolled his eyes at both of them. Lisa continued, her voice becoming more high-pitched as she spoke, as if she were becoming younger and younger. Anita quickly looked at Jared but continued to hold her arm next to Lisa's. She did not say anything. She looked at her and Lisa's arms and then at Jared, who just shook his head and said, "This is serious brown." It appeared as if Anita and Lisa didn't hear Jared, because they continued talking about chocolate and marshmallows.

What I saw as Anita's and Lisa's failure to hear or take up Jared's story was alleviated by Jared's success at getting others to respond in their own voices. Unfortunately, the writing for that day was not signed as notebooks were passed among different teenagers during the rehearsal. However, three teenagers wrote in response to the interaction:

> A human being can explode by holding so much anger inside or just certain things that irritate, haunts, or bothers them. A human being can lose their self control, or temper, and explode by being ticked off a lot or being hurt real badly emotionally. Some human beings can explode by being overwhelmed by things that they are not used to, hallucinating or just exaggerating things.
>
> A human being can only take so much. But none y'all don't hear me though.

Radical Noise, Gospel, Jazz Rhythm and Blues, Rap
Black Music.
Illegal . . . Distribute.
Illegal sale's distributed, sex, drugs.
Black Market.
Stock market crash.
Black!
The bad guys wear black. Objection your honor.
Evil mistress, black widow,
Followed by evil black shadow.
You think I don't know.
When disease wipes out millions of people. God is
   punishing us. God is black.
Santa is black.
You think I don't know. Self-conscience—psychology in
   reverse.
You think I don't know.
You think I do not know that everything you hear is
   black.

I am black and the world shall bow as I cross thy path
    for I am the one who
Brings bad luck.
Black Cat.

  No one cares what you have to say—at least no one in your com-
munity cares, because you keep pushing it in my face trying to shove it
down my throat that I am black, like I don't know that already.
  Your cameras.
  Your indifference.
  Do you care or do you want people to think you do?
  Why you keep on pushing me? A train going faster than my cha-
otic brain is all I see. Why? Okay! Who cares?
  Are you deprived, underprivileged? And yet those Jordans wouldn't
suggest it. No good will tags on your floor.
  A kiss up. Wanting to look bad in order to look good.

These responses complicated Jared's voice, adding complexity and even con-
tradiction to what he was saying and how Anita and Lisa were responding.
The responses appear empathetic, ironic, and indifferent, respectively, but
they all weave other voices into the mix. As such, there are multiple perspectives on what Jared, Lisa, and Anita were doing and saying.

DIALOGISM AND A THEORY OF LISTENING

Although he offers great possibilities for understanding and building human
relations, Bakhtin's understanding of human interaction, as Zen Radio shows,
is fraught with breakdowns, dangers, and contradictions. Importantly, none of
the TeenStreet instructors ever pushed the teenagers to reveal more than they
wanted to or to respond in ways they found uncomfortable. TeenStreet implicitly promotes a pedagogy of dialogism that builds on Bakhtin's theories by
making explicit voice development's contingency on listening, but also captures the belief that listening and responding are idiosyncratic, with response
not always needing to be verbalized. The incorporation of writing into Zen
Radio captured this explicitness for me, and also the fact that other language
use and mediational means are not eliminated as sources of dialogism.
  To empathize with another, if only for a brief moment, requires a conscious realization not only of one's authorship but also the limitations of that
authorship. Limitations arise in listening and trying to "get down" what others
are saying, knowing that what we do "get down" manifests itself in our own
voices. The conscious realization of one's definitive yet limited authorship

should not be left to chance but should be a goal of the interactions that take place among students and around texts as a way of ferreting out both overt and covert consciousness and the nature of storying.

The theory of listening arising from TeenStreet practice requires not only that the listener spatially and temporally ground herself in relation to others but also that she self-reflect on her grounding (its sum total, if you will) and on that relationship. The listener moves back and forth from her own perspective to others' perspectives, as noted at the beginning of this chapter in the description of Denise's and Elena's writing. The listener empathizes with others, reflects on her own perspective in relation to others', and responds in some way, even if it is to disagree or question what she hears. Describing this sort of self-reflection, Victor Turner (1974) wrote:

> If one were able to arrest the social process as though it were a motion film and were then to examine the "still," the coexisting social relations within a community, one would probably find that the temporary structures were incomplete, open-minded, unconsummated. . . . But if one had the science-fiction means of penetrating into the mind of the arrested actors, one would undoubtedly find in them, at almost any endopsychical level existing between full brightness of conscious attention and the darker strata of the unconscious, a set of ideas, images, concepts, and so on, to which one could attach the label "atemporal structures." These are models of what people believe they do, ought to do, or would like to do. (p. 36)

Such self-reflection is defined in its relation with others. In other words, because of our empathizing, we are self-reflective, positioned to make sense of our own existence in relation to others because of the uniqueness of experience and perspective that others bring to bear on our own experience and perspective. Our unique perspectives are placed alongside others' unique perspectives, and in that we respond. Yet we move forward in the world as one being among all beings, full of possibilities, and needing to respond—to hear—continually because we are not "arrested actors" but actors in the process of becoming.

EMERGING VOICES

A writing activity from my second year demonstrates the idea of voice arising from oneself and being placed alongside others' voices as part of a heteroglossia of voices. The teenagers created sentences using their and others' initials. The sentences reflected the writer's perspective of himself in the world. For example, Donna wrote: "Stealin' away y'old man's rum, a young player emerged." This straightforward sentence—one that creatively used the initial

Y in Yusuf's name to incorporate the word *old*—was discussed for its meaning and the ramifications of people's experiences on that meaning. The imagery of this sentence is one that appears common to teenagers. A teenager's place in the world is defined by her coming of age and the understanding of those experiences, including the social attraction of alcohol. Being a "player"—an actor in the world—often means appropriating that which seemingly makes someone else a player. Although the meaning of the sentence appears fairly clear-cut, what it meant for the "young player" and its various ramifications for the teenagers were matters of debate, ones that brought up a number of possible worlds, ones as different as "kids will be kids" and the implications of teenage alcoholism.

Thus, a sentence whose meaning to the author was clear-cut carries ramifications for the actors and experiencers of the imagery that go beyond the words themselves to incorporate the experiences of other teenagers. In writing this sentence, Donna gave voice to her understanding or experience. Yet, in interpretation, others' understanding came to the surface, making Donna aware of possible meanings her words can have for others and, in turn, her. Donna spoke from her own place and time and saw how others' listening recreated the sentence as meaning something different.

Bryn concluded the activity by summarizing the conversation about voice that was woven throughout the discussion. He asked what voice is. The teenagers offered ideas grounded in the self, such as "thought," "experience," "attitude," and "emotion." Voice, Bryn agreed, is something of one's own. Yet it is also something that is nurtured in interaction, as the activity demonstrated, often taking on meaning from others. Bryn said that voice includes "mood, rhythm, and a sense of self. It's like shifting out of yourself that which is you and putting it out there for others. It can come back and surprise you, though." I suggest that when it does come back it is someone else's voice, taking up words you had, in turn, taken up. And it is to that "coming back" that we must listen if our voices are to grow and be meaningful to ourselves and others.

DEFINING OURSELVES IN RELATION TO OTHERS

Bakhtin spoke of the fact that we cannot exist apart from others and that our existence is defined in relation to others'. The more we know about others' lives, the more we can say about our own. Conveying this understanding to students is the purpose of the theory of listening put into practice at TeenStreet. Social interaction is the focus of TeenStreet practice and needs to be a focus of classroom practice. In interaction, the self engages others' stories as full of possibilities, as full of nuances and more than the self can know on its own. As part of a theory of listening, others' stories inform my existence as possible reflections of the world and as codes of meaning, both hidden and revealed, that I must reflect on. While the self's interpretation of others' stories is unique and a re-creation of the stories, the self's understanding is limited to its own evolving perspective. It is others' stories and the self's reflection on them, as well as the self's own experiences, that move the self forward into the world. Thus, others' stories or perspectives and my interpretation of them help me make sense of the world.

IT'S ABOUT VOICE

No research on composition addresses fully what is happening at TeenStreet simply because TeenStreet is not about writing and writing instruction only. TeenStreet is about expression and communication. Writing, although an important part of the TeenStreet creative process, is only one part of it. In this regard, TeenStreet leaves me with these questions: Why aren't writing instruction and composition research overtly about everyday expression and communication instead of usually about an artificial, static, and seemingly, for many students, debilitating pedagogy? Why have we isolated writing from every other means of expression and the very lives of students we teach, including what we aspire to in human relations? If writing instruction and composition research over the last 2,500 years tell us anything, it is that talk about writing has been, for the most part, a ruse, with the mediational capacity of writing being treated, at best, as being of secondary importance.

To assume there are particular prewriting exercises or ways of prewriting, to assume there are particular ways of doing inquiry and revising, to even assume we can make enough of a distinction among writing genres to teach students how to write persuasively as opposed to narratively or expositorily, is to assume, in part, what it is a student's voice should be saying. Although these are not necessarily assumptions we should forego—after all, as teachers, we do have to assume to some degree what is best for our students—they are fertile with risks of forgetting who our students are and what they bring to the classroom, not only experientially but communicatively.

There are examples of writing instruction and composition research that focus on voice and contextualize writing as meaningful in students' lives (Arrastia, 1990; Bee, 1993; Cone, 1993a, 1993b; Fasheh, 1995; Griffith, 1982; McLeod, 1986; Searle, 1984). Much of this instruction and research over the last 30 years was derived from the work of Paulo Freire and critical theorists, as well as whole language proponents like Ken and Yetta Goodman, Frank Smith, and Don Graves. But like others, Freire's efforts, while garnering support, have not blossomed into full-scale responses to formalist writing instruction. Instead, the efforts of critical literacy teachers and researchers are like voices in the desert: Few people hear them, particularly as the winds of traditional instruction whip about. What is missing or has not been sustainable has much to do with James Gee and colleagues' (Gee et al., 1996) belief that critical literacy teachers and researchers have focused too much on critiquing literacy failures and not enough on ideas or agendas for positive change.

TeenStreet's creative process contributes to ideas and agendas for positive change by helping teenagers reconceptualize themselves not only as writers and artists but also as agents in the world. As agents, the teenagers use writing as a means of expression and communication. Their agency is contingent on interacting and understanding others' voice and on exploring possible existences either as characters they create or through imaginal interactions with others' images. These possible existences arise from the teenagers' experiences but go beyond those experiences in that in participating in the various TeenStreet exercises and in creating a script, the experiences interact and are interpreted from different perspectives and thus create new possibilities. The script, ultimately, stands apart from the teenagers' experience as something unique, something infused with multiple voices. In this sense, the teenagers are creating new culture—new reality—and thus are effective instigators of change.

7

The World Through Different Eyes

Bryn spoke of creating a revolutionary experience between people when writing, making writing itself a luminal experience. Writing has the capability of putting a person on the threshold between self and other, between what is and what is possible. Luminality, indeed, is that state of existence where possibilities run amok, where we can be who we want to be, where our voices are a symphony of sounds made singular in their uniqueness. This notion of possibilities, of luminality, and of writing functioning within imaginal interaction was essential to helping the teenagers at TeenStreet reconceptualize writing, creativity, and their understanding of what it means to be agents in the world.

Bryn also spoke of verbalizing possibilities and not categories and taxonomies of existence, or as he called it, "not buying off the shelf" or simply appropriating others' ways of knowing and communicating. What he meant, I think, is not to get caught up in what others say, or buy into the glibness that is easily accessible. Instead, one should work within oneself from one's own time and place and respond to others from one's own perspective.

The awareness of self and the necessity of interaction that defines the movement and improvisation activities at TeenStreet transform individual writing into a use of language that is one's own even as we draw on others in our understanding. Integral to such language use is expressing oneself fully and understandably to others. Bryn cast writing in these terms, pointing out that what the teenagers are asked to do is hard work that takes a constant relooking and rethinking, if only because everyone is in the process of living. Yet the entire writing process at TeenStreet is premised on the notion of looking, hearing, relooking, and rehearing. This chapter presents the teenagers' understanding of this process.

WORKING THE TENSIONS

The TeenStreet creative process challenged teenagers' notions of writing, ones usually developed in school. The movement, improvisation, voice, and writing activities helped teenagers reconceptualize their notions about artistry and creativity, human interaction, and the relationship of self and other. Things they may never have considered doing when interacting became habitual after a few months of workshops and rehearsals. Many teenagers said they were transferring these newfound notions to their lives outside the ensemble studio. After only two weeks of rehearsals, most of the teenagers during both years I was a participant-observer made distinctions between writing they do in school and writing they do during rehearsals, and between how they were encouraged to act at TeenStreet and how they felt their actions were confined outside TeenStreet. They all spoke about the emotional bases that guide all the activities at TeenStreet.

For the first time, many teenagers said, they were expressing who they are in their writing and really thinking about what it was they wanted to do creatively beyond TeenStreet. For example, Yusuf noted that most of the writing he did before TeenStreet "didn't have any type of emotional connection. It was more appearance, how your paper looked and how good it sounded, instead of . . . is there any depth to it." Denise said she had never "written from emotion" until joining TeenStreet. She joined the ensemble during one of its summer workshops and was returning after being away for a year. She told me how the process of "letting go," of allowing her experiences to enter into the writing, took time to develop.

> Even after that first summer I felt like I really hadn't let go. I felt like there was a lot of stuff I was holding back. I was writing some things from honesty but there was still things I wasn't. I mean, you'd go back to school and you'd go back to the same way, writing things in the same pattern, bullshitting through papers.

She described TeenStreet exercises as "writing from sincere emotions." "School," she said, "somehow takes it and makes it clinical."

I interviewed Yusuf and Denise together, which allowed their thoughts about creativity and writing to interact, as each often picked up on what the other said. Early in our conversation, Denise pointed out the significance of art, particularly dancing, in her life, saying that art is "a total expression of life." Yusuf said, "Art is paraphrasing life."

I then asked Yusuf how writing fit into his life, particularly his understanding of it before TeenStreet and now, after four months of rehearsals. Many of the teenagers grappled with what it means to be a writer or an artist in another medium. For them, the communicative potential of writing and other artistic endeavors was something they were only beginning to realize. At the same time, the tension created by competing or conflicting Discourses—in Yusuf's case, school versus TeenStreet—was evident and used as a source of exploration. Yusuf, in his writing, actions, and this interview, made an effort to work those tensions.

> *YUSUF*: When I first came to TeenStreet, this is one of the first things I
> told Ron, okay, I have a problem because I am okay in English in
> school and because they always taught . . . I don't know if they
> taught you to have boundaries, but I do know that there is a stan-
> dard way of writing, that you have rules which you follow and that
> you have an F if you don't follow these rules, and when I came to
> TeenStreet, it was like, "Okay, just write, you don't have to do any
> boundaries, you don't have to do anything. You're free from all re-
> strictions and don't edit yourself," and all these other things which
> just confused me so much because I had been having a hard time
> learning all these rules and it's like, "Don't do them." There is a
> time and a place when to do them, but he said just don't do them
> at first. I think . . . I find it a lot . . . I find it a lot useful when I
> write the way I want to write. I'll write the standard way of writing
> when I want to communicate with other people, but, you know,
> just with me . . .
> *CHRIS*: Well, you don't think you can communicate with just writing
> the way you do here?
> *YUSUF*: Yeah, I do. I do, but I think it's that people have to listen
> harder . . .
> *CHRIS*: Everyone has written in here . . . I mean, has communicated
> something, no?
> *YUSUF*: I mean that most people don't want to listen to that. I mean
> you really have to put out effort to listen when it comes to the writ-
> ing in here. Other writing you just read it and it's like, "Okay,

okay." I have a hard time having an emotional connection to that type of writing because it seems like you're not saying anything.

CHRIS: What kind of writing is that?

YUSUF: I mean school, standard writing, not prose . . .

DENISE: Four sentences, two paragraphs . . .

YUSUF: Yeah, all those that they say standard English is.

CHRIS: Well, do you think they are right?

YUSUF: Uh, well, see I still have double standards for me. Writing, I have not been doing too long. I like to write. Then I started rapping and that was writing, and it was writing for me that, at first, wasn't any different thing because everybody was doing it, and then when I started doing it actually for myself, that's when it starts making a difference. I do need to learn what it is they teach you in school because, you know, you do have to communicate with the world. And so that's what I'm learning that for. But to express myself, to express what's in my heart or whatever, that's when I write whatever comes out.

CHRIS: Don't you think you can do both? Don't you think that there's a way of expressing yourself that communicates?

YUSUF: Yeah, but it's easier just writing the way that you want. You know I'm going to, when I say that I'm going to learn how to write standard, that includes learning how to, you know, learning what writing is and that automatically I'm going to express myself the way I want to express myself. Now, I find it easier to write the way I want to write. It's just easier. It's probably just laziness. But I'm going to learn. I'm not saying I don't know how to write. I mean, when I say I'm going to learn how to write I mean having an emotional connection with what I'm writing when I'm trying to express myself in a paper and everything, which is one of the harder things for me.

CHRIS: Well, do you think you have an emotional connection with writing for school? Do you think it's possible to express your feelings to someone else? And do you think schools teach that?

YUSUF: I think that they . . . I don't think . . . I can't say all schools . . .

CHRIS: What about your experience?

YUSUF: Well, most of the writing I have done didn't have any type of emotional connection. It was more appearance, how your paper looked and how good it sounds, instead of . . . of . . . is there any depth to it. And I say it kind of how you say it but it's much more what you say, and if you listen to what I say you'll get much more from it. I mean, that is the whole purpose of writing, to communicate what you feel to someone else. But I think there is still a lot of things . . . I mean, my only problem was . . . I don't mean to drag this out . . . My only problem was there are things you don't have to say because you can express things between two people without really saying them, and I like to leave things that don't need to be said unsaid because they're a lot deeper to me because like we have a relationship and it's something that we both know, it's a feeling and then we have to search for words to define that feeling or the best way to express that but we already know it but we have to find a way to express that to someone who doesn't have that feeling. It's like me and you already have it and that's what's important.

CHRIS: Well, some people might say that that's what good writing is: Touching other people's emotions without having to put everything out there, without actually saying everything, and having others jump into your words and say, "Yeah, I haven't had the same experience but I understand that experience . . . "

YUSUF: I have a lot of respect for writers.

Such distinctions between writing done for school and writing done for Teen-Street were common among the teenagers, although I do not think anyone grappled more with them than Yusuf.

More significantly, however, Yusuf's comments reflect the tension between experience and language, and how for him experience takes precedence over language and language cannot always speak to what he feels or experiences. He, however, spoke of learning how to use language in ways that could help burnish his feelings and experiences for others. He saw this ability as indicative of good writing, an ability to express oneself in ways communicable to others. Yusuf's yearning for relationships that transcend language have not lessened his need to develop voice if he wants to communicate with more than only those people attuned to his experience.

EXPLORING POSSIBILITIES

Denise, during the same interview, said her TeenStreet experience influenced her understanding of dance in this way:

I got in the summer program, and it was like we traveled all over the city in a hot van and did this piece that we created and it was my first, I guess, real creative writing, acting project. I had been dancing up until then. I mean TeenStreet is totally, TeenStreet has changed the way I thought about my art in many ways because dance can be pretty clinical

when you study it to the bone and try to dissect names and try to be exact, and a lot of dance loses emotions—a lot of dances don't have it to
begin with—and like I say no one can teach that and it started me to
think, like Ron is forever . . . one of the buzzwords around TeenStreet is
"emotional connection." He has been saying that since I've been working here and probably since time began. . . . [Working with TeenStreet]
has taught me to let things happen and let them come up and if they
do then so what. When I'm choreographing, I let the same thing happen, and when I'm teaching I let the same thing happen. . . . I mean
you can't teach that to someone, but you can give them an arena to let
that happen. . . . There are so few places in a person's life where someone is going to say, "Okay, just go crazy. Jump off the walls and scratch
your eyes out." . . . This just gives you so many opportunities to learn
about yourself, to explore yourself. And then you're able to take that
out and put it into real life.

Similar to what Denise said, Nick saw TeenStreet as providing a forum
to experiment and delve into who he is. He noted during an interview that he
had a good opportunity to learn how to write in school, but that he "kind of
blew it off" because "it didn't seem important at the time because it wasn't
what my life was about." Now, he said, there are many things he can do
creatively that include writing, things he had never thought of before. He
watched the first rehearsal from the chairs, telling me months later that he was
"freaked" by what was going on, although he felt he understood the purpose of
the exercises. "I just couldn't see myself doing it," he said, referring to the
movement exercises. Now he looks for ways of incorporating the same expressiveness and experimentation that he experienced during rehearsals into his
artistic projects outside TeenStreet.

When I asked him how TeenStreet affected his drumming and music
development, Nick said:

Well, it's definitely all positive as far as, well, when I think about things,
shit, like what I think about what I'm going to do, about this thing, career this and career that, and knowing that stuff like this exists is pretty
good even if I never consider continuing this outside of here. Even the
stuff I've learned in here has tied over to my drums and my outlook on
performance. . . . Like not holding back ideas. It's like I still am holding
back ideas, like when I go up on stage all I do is play drums. I have
hopes of incorporating some of this stuff, like expanding upon that. I
can expand my drum playing and that's great, but there is so much to
do outside of that. I think that's what TeenStreet has opened my eyes

to. It's like knowing that that's there too, and that it's a possibility and that I can do stuff like this and write my own stuff.

Yusuf, too, saw what was happening at TeenStreet as an awakening to what is possible artistically and communicatively. "This [TeenStreet creative process] is another option. It affects the way I look at the world."

Tonya, a self-proclaimed short story writer, poet, and journal writer, called TeenStreet freedom compared with school, although she was a successful student in one of Chicago's more prestigious parochial schools. Sheila, Tonya's close friend and classmate, concurred. As the workshops wound down and the business of fine-tuning the script and blocking the performance took place, Tonya told Bryn and me about a paper she was writing for a school assignment. Rehearsal had not started yet, and the three of us and Sheila were sitting on stage. Tonya jumped to her feet and danced across the floor, reminding me of Ty that first day I walked up the stairs to the stage. She danced back to where the rest of us sat. She had so much tension to burn off, she said, because she was writing a report on *Dr. Faustus* and had only three weeks to do it, which, she said as she backed toward the middle of the stage, was not enough time. Sheila agreed, saying she was doing a report on *The Picture of Dorian Gray* and she was not finished yet, either.

Tonya's expressiveness that morning was unusual. She, more than any of the other teenagers, had extensive experience performing, having sung in church choirs and state recital competitions. Yet she more than anyone else in that year's ensemble was always being reminded by Ron to experiment with her singing and take chances in her movement and writing.

"We had to read critics," she said, as if that was evidence enough of her disgust for the assignment. "I was looking all over the place, especially the Internet, for information." She again started jumping around. Sheila smiled. Bryn and I laughed even as we tried to empathize with Tonya's plight.

"Other classes had a lot more time to do the assignment," Sheila said.

Tonya nodded her head in agreement, coming to a stop at the edge of the stage and in front of us. "Yeah, and I went off on that Faustus, tying him into modern life—about people who befriend you and are the devil, entice you and then lead you astray," she said, serious now.

Sheila agreed, nodding her head and looking at Bryn and me.

"I told the teacher what *I* thought about the story," Tonya said. She and Sheila presented a litany of problems they had writing their reports, including computer breakdowns, lack of time, and Internet problems. ("A lot of that stuff was in German," Tonya said.) But they agreed that the books they read were good. Tonya started jumping around again and acting as if she were playing the drums.

"She's acting crazy," Sheila said.

Tonya heard this and slowed down to consider what Sheila had said. Momentarily, she said with a smirk on her face, "Ron says I'm acting like he has been trying to get me to act for four months. I'm acting the way I should."

Ron never talked about how the teenagers should act. Instead, he talked about not letting others confine their actions. He talked about being uninhibited and expressive, about being responsive to others and responsible for oneself and others. Although many of the teenagers expressed this as being able to cut loose and act crazy, the goals of a project-based activity, where multiple stories are synthesized into one script, made the TeenStreet experience for many teenagers the most demanding they ever had. During the two years I was at TeenStreet, only one person quit because of dissatisfaction with her ensemble experience. Others, like Mona, Cheryl, Donna, and Tonya, left because of personal reasons. Invariably, about a quarter of the teenagers audition for a second or even third year. About three-quarters continue their artistic pursuits beyond TeenStreet.

Other members of the ensemble voiced similar transformations to Tonya's, where they became more expressive of their own understanding of the world. They also spoke of how they approached life outside TeenStreet, particularly creative endeavors, differently, whether it was Nick, Karen, and Charles and their music; Anthony and his painting; Denise and her dancing; or Sharon and her feelings about her expressiveness being confirmed by her TeenStreet experience. She told me she had always approached life in ways promoted by TeenStreet. She was amazed to find a place that confirmed her beliefs about creativity and expressiveness. She also said she has tried to transfer what she has learned at TeenStreet to her writing at school. She told Bryn and me how her English teacher commented to her that her writing "'really tells a story.' It's the first time he's really taken an interest in what I'm saying, asking me things like what I mean by *this* or *that*."

Indeed, for many of the teenagers, their newfound understanding of creativity and well-honed dedication often carried over to their writing and its uses. Tonya's story demonstrates how she was now using writing in school. Others made similar comments. Sheila, during a discussion with Bryn about a line she had written, said of her own writing: "It's like I am a real silent person in a way. I have all this stuff in me but I'm scared to let it out. I'm now realizing that it can be used as a silent strength rather than trying to turn it away. . . . I got so many things in me and I don't understand. . . . There is so much. I need to learn how to separate them." Elena said this about her TeenStreet experience: "Before, if I would write it's like something I would write, like a story like, 'She went to the store and her mother argued with her.' Now, it's like I write more freely. I write like from my mind. I try to create more. Free Street has broken me out of that self-consciousness [about writing]."

Of his own transformation, Yusuf said:

In this program alone, I've been given a lot of titles. He [Ron] called me a singer one day, and he called me an actor, he called me a writer, and so now, it's like wow. I would like to do it, and it's helped me in school because in school the first couple of times we were writing they'd say you have to write like this. We have guidelines and rules and process, like they say you have to follow a, b, c, d, and e, and he [Bryn] came in and told us to write whatever, go, to let that go, to write whatever, to do this [points at a pile of his writing and the script draft]. This has helped me in my writing because I have to follow those same guidelines but this has helped me with my creativity when I have to think about what I have to write about and how to get to that idea. Now, I love to actually write. I've started to write poetry, rap. I'd like to use it for the enlightenment of somebody.

Yusuf's comment about being given a lot of titles is reminiscent of Bryn's proclamation that the teenagers are Master Poets and that they must remember that regardless of what others say. Similarly, Ron, Bryn, and Anita made it a priority to talk about the uniqueness of each teenager's perspective and the power of their voices. Ron often spoke of glorious failure, meaning for the teenagers to take risks and not be afraid of failure.

STRUGGLES WITH THE WORD AND THE WORLD

The significance of writing, and other mediational means such as music and painting, in many of the teenagers' lives went beyond merely being told and, thus, thinking they were now writers or artists of a particular caliber. The impression I got in speaking with the teenagers and in watching them work during workshops and rehearsals was that writing, and creativity, was a means to something more valuable. Writing, like oral language, became a means of addressing the world, both communicating their own lives and coming to understand others'. The teenagers spoke of their struggles with writing, and TeenStreet did not lessen those struggles; it just changed their nature. The teenagers now struggled to communicate their existence and contemplated in their writing and aloud what they wanted writing to do for them.

Few struggled with writing while trying to claim it as something valuable for communicating who they are as much as Chau. As noted in Chapter 4, English was her second language, and she had difficulty with English grammar, particularly in her school writing. Chau's TeenStreet writing, however, was descriptive and reflective, with her problems in grammar not impeding her communicative ability. Bryn recognized her struggle and did not minimize it. After going over some of her writing and letting her talk about what she meant, he suggested that she only needed to relook at what she writes to ferret out the meaning of some of her unique phrasings.

Not everyone claimed a new writing life because of their TeenStreet experience. Tony struggled with writing, and told me a year after he left Teen-Street that he seldom writes. An aspiring dancer who teaches in the Chicago Park District and helps choreograph the TeenStreet dance numbers, Tony said he has to force himself to write down choreography notes. "If anything," he said, "Ron did teach me that about writing. I need it to teach dance."

During a rehearsal early in my first year, after we had broken into groups to write, Tony refused to participate, saying simply, "You go ahead. I'll just tell you my story when you're ready." I never saw Tony write more than a few lines. I asked Ron about this, and he said that although Tony can read and write, "he is well below grade level." Ron blamed the schools Tony attended, noting that he went to an arts-based high school where he never had to read or write simply because he was into dance and theater. "Do you believe that?" Ron said. "He is a great dancer, but what is holding him back is not his dancing." Tony dropped out of a downtown university his sophomore year.

To see Tony teach dance, however, is to see a master teacher in action. He moves from instructing to mentoring to watching his students perform with an ease that marks him as being at home with what he is doing. He welcomes his students into that home. He is always talking and moving, always praising and making suggestions. He is always experimenting. Holding an open hand to his chin, he will stop everything to reflect on what is happening or what needs to happen. "How 'bout if we try this?" he will say, and then dance. "What do you think? Does that work? What do you think we should do?"

In talking to Tony, I got the impression that he had no interest in writing. He admitted its difficulty, saying he just does not see it as a talent of his. At the same time, Tony asked to see what I was writing about TeenStreet. "I want to see what you say about me," he said. I gave him an early draft and later, when I asked what he thought, he said it was good and he enjoyed reading it, admitting however that he only glanced through most of it looking for his pseudonym.

Tony exudes confidence in his abilities, particularly his dancing ability and his power of persuasion. He is very personable. He was quick to tell me that his personality made school easier for him. "The teachers loved me," he said. "I was involved in everything." I came to see Tony's lack of writing ability to be a lack of interest more than anything else.

Tony is literate in many ways, particularly in ways related to dance and performance. I do not doubt that he struggles with writing and, for that reason, may be alienated from it. Tony's choice is not to use literacy in ways marked out by others. Literacy is a tool that Tony believes he does not need to use any more than he already does. With Tony, I heard Denise's refrain that she is not a writer but a dancer. Yet, although Denise came to relish the opportunity to express herself in writing, Tony continued to reject the idea even as it related to being a dancer. Tony personifies the idea that creative and communicative ability are not dependent on or reflective of literacy ability or use, or one's own well-being or self-realization.

I wanted to end with Tony's story to reiterate, ironically in a way, literacy's mediational capacity and what literacy can do for us. I wanted to recontextualize literacy as a mediation tool with many possible uses, both quantitatively and qualitatively, with its greatest value being how it makes accessible our own and others' stories. Tony shared in this use at TeenStreet. As a member of the ensemble and, later, as dance instructor, he was an important contributor to imaginal interaction and, therefore, to the activity that is TeenStreet.

ON THE CUSP OF WHAT IS POSSIBLE

For other teenagers, the surprise in their voices at how different writing is at TeenStreet is a result of approaching and using writing as a way of communicating their experiences and learning and drawing upon those of others. The difference between writing at TeenStreet and many of the teenagers' understanding of writing outside the ensemble is in their developing conception of what writing can do for them and others. The teenagers take ownership of the words they write because it is a language borne of themselves, expressing their consciousness, both overt and covert. TeenStreet fosters an understanding of literacy premised on intuition. All knowledge is understood to precipitate from experience, either real or vicarious. What others offer, what the world offers, builds on that experience.

More significantly than changing conceptions and uses of writing, however, is the realization among the teenagers of the importance of their and others' lived experiences and the need to communicate those experiences regardless of the mediational means chosen. The movement, improvisation, voice, and writing activities in and of themselves are not what make the TeenStreet creative process successful and transformative. Although all the activities are important to what the ensemble does and to what the teenagers become, it is the reconceptualization of the self–other relationship through the use of the activities, through imaginal interaction, as image-(re)creating structures that is most significant. Putting teenagers on the cusp of what is possible in their existence is what TeenStreet is about. As a community intent on creating a professional ensemble script, the ensemble is rich in possibilities. The image-(re)creating structures, the movement and improvisation activities, allow teenagers to draw on experience and to fuse images and language in transformative ways. Bruner (1986) called this fusion *narrative knowing*, which, he states, allows us to identify ourselves and others in the world. Of this, Fleckenstein (1996) wrote that the language of narrative knowing allows us to "traffic in possibilities and perspectives, not in certainties" (p. 927). Who has not felt the power of narrative that emanates from or settles within one's being, making one shudder with a newfound understanding or revelation, with a sudden realization of possibilities and perspectives unthought or unfelt before? One can feel these possibilities within one's bones, right down to the last cell on the big toe.

Appendix

Body House:
A Jazz Tricycle

© 1997

by TeenStreet

Facilitated by Ron Bieganski

directed by Ron Bieganski
assistant director: Anita Evans
musical direction: Mars Williams
choreography: Happi Price and Ron Bieganski
costumes: Ann Boyd

*writers: Griffin Rodriquez, Diana Campos, Rom Chy,
Zach Fiocca, Karla Galva, Meka Hayes, Shanel Jackson,
Gyasi Kress, Alex Present, Ron Bieganski, Anita Evans*

Body House: A Jazz Tricycle

(1997)
(STEPPENWOLF)

CHARLES—I respect the sub-harmonic frequencies of the bass. When I caught the beat, it was bumping and pounding like the sea. I remember my first time—spoiled little tantrums of childish waves and quakes. I understand the constriction of stillness. Down and out. Down and out. Just hang, but don't give up.

YUSUF—The first time? Let me slide on down that memory. Images. Images. It's a slide show. Everybody wants to know what I do. Same thing as you.

DENISE—No one holds my hand when I cross the street anymore.

Elephant Chicano men with dicks like log anchors charged at me with their horny insistence. Though my blood is their blood—their compassion unzipped with their flies.

Like I said, no one holds my hand anymore.

ANTHONY—My number one time. Clocks Tick Tock. Crack—Tick Tock. (*laughter*) That gave me a little Jesus for a moment. I like someone. Push-me. Pull-you. I should ask her out. Run it down. I can't ask her out, I don't have much money right now. I'm in a transition.

CHAU—I had a dream once that I had a baby with Big Bird and it had yellow feathers on its head. I watch too much TV?

I learned English when I first got to this country by watching *Sesame Street*. As I watched Bert and Ernie I realized the only truth is in the alphabets.

LISA—A B C. That's all the truth you'll get from me.

VIOLIN—With my pain all ablaze I turned to the left.

BLUE H—Let's all talk about sex. Talk talk. You're talking Blue. Bet you want to know. My mom would kill me and you, if she even knew you asked me. She's probably going through my bedroom looking for clues. One hundred dependent souls depend on my mother's sacred independence. Triggering those senses, and I deal with my mom's consequences.

SUPER LADY—My dear Watson . . . I want to play the game just to play the game.

145

Got to climb fast up the hill. Trip of goats Kid. That's a trip of goats. Jump. Jump.

A boyfriend would actually be O.K., but I'm fighting crime today.

GUY UMMER—My first time? Doing what . . . Rogeeea bow motions. You know—Rogeeea bow motions.

My first time . . . you know the usual. You know. "Blue H" is sleeping with her rump couched over there—Ask her. I heard about the time you tried to hit it! I love you. I love you. I really do—Kissey poo.

I've had a lot of girl friends—lots of them. Crap. Snap. Ping. I would like to meet someone I like. Crap. Snap Ping.

I feel like Hank Bukouski before Fill Taylor knew how to read. Next question please!

CYCLE 1

YUSUF (TROMBONE)—Look at me eyes all shut up, face contorted like you're trapped in your body house.

CHARLES (STRASS)—(*music intro . . .*)

VIOLIN—(*after Nick comes in out*) And I fell out of my world.

TERRI (SUPER LADY)—Something is sucking up my hugging family. (*Twister*)

SHARON (BLUE HA)—She is there, with her loud red stockings on and her pink Thoughts. She is passing notes in school.

She has lost the sound.

She can't find middle "C" anymore.

She thought she didn't need her voice teacher.

She doesn't care.

She is a full born puppy.

She is a beginner.

TERRI—I was mad when my sister got sucked up. Now another sister! I will try to finger out what is happening.

That's why I became "Sherlock Holmes Rapper Super Lady."

ANTHONY (WATSON)—Who?

TERRI—I am Sherlock Holmes Rapper Super Lady creeping to finger out what was sucking up my hugging family.

I found a clue in the dirt, my sisters were sucked up, I believe by a twister.

ANTHONY—Let's go find a twister.

TERRI—Because of my sisters, Super Lady will discover things violently. Super Lady will chase people while creeping. . . . Super Lady is always curious.

ANTHONY—Sherlock Holmes Rapper Super Lady.

TERRI—I eat, jump, and hug at the same time. I talk and mess with people. I am powerful, because I can fly.

I am different, because I can fight with my "business mind."

I never pace.

ANTHONY—Never. She fingers things out. Sherlock Holmes Rapper Super Lady.

SHARON—It must have been a part of her, long before, because all it took was a soft breath in her ear. Less effort than the unthinkable, the automatic. To get that little part of her growing till it was her, or she was it, or either or rather.

Better you realize that small things can ruin the world or your world, or your big small world. All that surrounds the world, or all that surrounds an atom, or either or rather.

Maybe it's better if she don't remember her dreams. Dreams stop the feeling in her body for a moment. She don't like that feeling. . . . Sorry.

TERRI—There is a speed limit and there are some people who attempt to travel at the speed of God. *(snap fingers)* That's the speed of God.

YUSUF—You like speed.

SHARON—I don't like limits.

TERRI—Do you see this? The twister approached around here.

DENISE (MOVE)—What do you want?

YUSUF—No touchy. No touch no one. This is a comparison: A feather is an S.O.S. pad in this world. *(whisper)*

SHARON—Don't whisper.

YUSUF—Listen kid, trip of Goats kid, no amigo Chico kid.

I can explained the rhythm of dirt.

DENISE—You're an old man at 19 with an aged mind.

He just toys with the idea of friendship.

YUSUF—Sweaty woman, Sweaty girl . . .

Sweaty girl wants to feel like a sweaty woman, is that it?

SHARON—Your eyeballs full of red hots.

TERRI—Dirty tears surfaced on her fudge skin.

SHARON—*(a silent gulp of air)*

CHARLES—Triggering senses and dealing with the consequences.

YUSUF—Whoooo, slide your way down the memory.

TERRI—A young lion tears apart her fabric of reality.

ANTHONY—Was she in love?

TERRI—Listen to the rhythm.

CHAU (FLAP)—The only truths that exist are in the alphabets.

DENISE—Don't try and tell me about dedication, devotion, sincere undying love feeeeeelings that come from some place so deep.

YUSUF—Sit in it, Sit. Climb through it. Chase it.

NICK (GUY UMMER)—
Bow clear Paper hear
Wire pon pon threw.
Wait. Go Go. Wait Go.
Through it, run it,
Stick stick stick.
Rogeeea bow motions.
Push me—pull you.
Run it down.

SHARON—Walls are hard. Windows are hard.
Especially when you're trying to go through.

YUSUF—I Checked every wall for a soft spot. Now try the windows. Check every one. One, two . . . I'm going in search of two hearts.

DENISE—Let's go.

SHARON—How the F can I leave. One hundred dependent souls depend on my sacred independence. This is something I learned on *Sesame Street*: "Today's show is sponsored by the letter F and the number zero to represent my tired life." *(close eyes—trapped in her body house)*

DENISE—Listen kid you don't touch him and you don't know where his ABC's have been.

YUSUF—Can everyone say "Asshole" . . . good boys and girls. Look at me. Eyes all shut up. Face contorted like you're trapped in your "body house."

SHARON—Maybe if I was someone else this would be easier. I heard the wind whisper to me, that going naked might be my best disguise.

NICK—Crap. Snap. Tap. Like toes pop ping pain. . . . Pain. . . . look over those? Who me? . . . Can you feel, is it for real, Someone steer the wheel . . .

DENISE—Go on move Faith to a new day.

YUSUF—Forget the crap that they say, "believe in thy-self."

TERRI—Someone whispered about going in search of two hearts.

ANTHONY—You can find old whispers in the dirt?

TERRI—It's about two hearts?

DENISE—It was Honey marinated sperm that awakened his sleeping sex.
Spotlights of lust and beds full of pain.
Cheddar cheese and buttered popcorn.
Sour patch kids and friendship bracelets.
Kids begging for macaroni.

SHARON—
4 kids to a bed and roaches as pets
3 shards of families and 1 dying generation.
12 locks on the door and 3 knives under your mattress.
24 kids shot in drive byes and 2 minds full of dreams.

TERRI—She got inspired and immediately stopped her journey, right here, on this spot to light up her arm and head . . . the fire lit up the darkness—that comforts her loneliness.

YUSUF—5, 10, 15, 20 I have a dime, a dime in my pocket. Rolling' around with a tantrum on my mind. . . .

SHARON— . . . 05, 10, 15, 20 . . .

YUSUF—Triggering senses and dealing with the consequences.
   Clocks Tick Tock, Come on . . . make a decision? Crack Tick Tock, Crack Tick Clocks Tick Tock . . .

NICK—Tick Tock clack, Tick tock crack. Tock. Tick Crack.

SHARON—I is olate? I is olate? Olate is? Is-olate. Isolated? . . . Isolated.

YUSUF—You're It.

TERRI—Touch Down. The twister touched down right here.

(THE EVENT)

SHARON—I twist. You twist, we twist.

YUSUF—Whisper in my ear, sing me songs of love.

SHARON—Ooh I'm digging' you.

YUSUF—Snap your fingers. Fill all my dreams of you digging me.

SHARON—Ohh I'm digging you.

YUSUF—Take me to a room of lust and lies from all those other times.

SHARON—Mama tell me what he wants so I can give him more.

YUSUF—Rub your fingers down my . . .

SHARON—Ohhh I'm digging you. Tell me I'm beautiful. Steal my innocence. Damn he's digging me.

(THE BIG—E)

TERRI—An earthquake breaks—stillness is found. There's just the breaths of a mountain or two. Right here.
   Stillness. This stillness was 8.2 on the Richter scale.

(AFTER SHOCK)

SHARON—I . . . so . . . lated. I . . . so . . . lated. I . . . so . . . lated. She is iso-lated.

ANTHONY—You move so gracefully, almost as if you had buttered your feet.

SHARON—Nothing more than thunder, darkness, clouds, this disrupt to heaven, man, woman. . . . Me.

TERRI—Always else where! I had a dream that flying Sherlock Holmes Rapper Super Lady couldn't steer when she flew.

NICK—Steer the wheel.

TERRI—I was caught up in a tree. But I was Super Lady! I have to creep to finger out what was sucking up my family.

ANTHONY—So many questions.

TERRI—Questions are baggage . . . and Baggage can only weigh one down. I want to move like a mind.

I will finger things out with a bursting army of mind.

DENISE—Release, release. Kill his ass. Take him by the neck and squeeze until you break the bass and fall out the window.

SHARON—No more cries leaking through the holes in my aching ears. I'm a Brave heart searching for peace. A,   B,   C,   D. . . . Mommy, sister, brother, please hear me.

DENISE—I hear. At the edge of the sun there's a pool with a diving board and a juice bar. Jump. Plunge into emptiness with no daily appointments. . . . Just one big open cattle call. That's a big dick of a headache going down.

CHAU—Hear, see, smell, touch, taste.

ANTHONY—More than 5 senses guide the unconscious. Right?

TERRI—What's wrong with you. We're looking for love.

ANTHONY—Yea.

SHARON—No touchy. No touch no one.

This is a comparison: A feather was an S.O.S. pad in that world. *(whisper)*

DENISE—Don't whisper to me.

SHARON—This won't rhyme or tell a story. This isn't something my Mama made me memorize to impress you.

YUSUF—Triggering senses and dealing with the consequences are you?

CHARLES—Figure it out. *(play notes—A   B   C   D   E   F   G . . .)*

SHARON—He is many things, never could explain them to no one. I'm holding court four stories above a pretty thin book.

DENISE—Balance, you're short of it.

SHARON—I understand. I really do understand the full movement of moving and the stillness of restriction.

TERRI—Blood rushes to my head with so little awareness that I'm in the middle of a thought. Where is it Watson?

ANTHONY—Love is a mystery. When it's solved I bet it vanishes.

SHARON—Now I know my ABC's.

YUSUF—5,   10,   15,   20. Rolling around with a tantrum on my mind. It wasn't that bad.

SHARON—I had a dream. I was walking down the street. My tummy was hurting. The people I was carrying inside would not stop fighting. I was yelling at my tummy while walking down the street. People. People was looking at me like I was crazy. They just didn't know it was a riot going on inside of me. The little people was just babies. How could they be so rowdy?

I got on the bus, the babies calmed down. I was calm. Until one of them kicked me. I jumped up and said that's it! I took a knife from my pocket and cut open my tummy. I grabbed one of the babies and started to choke the shit out of him. People on the bus was looking at me like, like I was crazy. I stopped, stared at the people and said what you looking at. I took a stapler from my pocket and stapled the babies back inside. I looked up and just walked off the bus. Behind me on the bus an old lady said "You an asshole." You're an asshole!

YUSUF—Maybe it's better if you don't remember your dreams.

SHARON—I am here, with my loud red stockings on and my pink Thoughts.

I'm passing notes in school.

I have lost the sound.

I can't find middle "C" anymore.

I thought I didn't need my voice teacher.

I don't care.

I'm a full-born puppy.

I'm a beginner.

YUSUF—Maybe if you were someone else this would be easier. Going naked might be your best disguise.

SHARON—Listen kid, no amigo Chico kid. No touchy, no touch no one.

NICK—Now, now, now, sound sound sound. Red red face face face. No more . . . more. Redun. Redoune. Redone. Redone. Redundant.

SHARON—With my pain all ablaze I turned to the left. . . .

YUSUF—A B C

CHARLES—(*play scale—A B C D E F G . . .*)

TERRI—There's no more clues.

SHARON—And I fell out of my world.

POSSESSION SEQUENCE

(*Musician Stay Lisa*
1. *Dis Eased clump*
2. *Clump around Sharon*
3. *watusi begins, Denise solo comes out of this and is focus; everybody else is backup*
4. *musician leaves [Yusuf, Lisa, Sharon, or Charles]*
5. *freeze frame called by Yusuf, Denise repeats a movement and the rest copy and watusi goes on*)

ANTHONY—I'm riding waves of emotions like a K-Mart toy. Stick a quarter in me. Wind up tears tell a story to destroy. But I'm safe.

My ass itches and my face burns. Finally given the chance to hug even
for a crack in time. Ice sculpture foreplay, like deep kissing the deep sea.
    So, I had an affair with anger that filled me with bug filled ice cubes
and beef jerky mold. . . . While she's off playing. Watson. Watson. Watson.
Watson. Watson.

(6. 3rd musician leaves
  7. antline with Yusuf leading
  8. Nick's possession begins [1.5 minutes to give birth to yourself]
  9. Bird Formation is called by Sharon behind Nick for 10 secs. Back to Ant-
  line with Yusuf leading. He calls this . . .
10. Nick's first words only
11. Back wall
12. Cycle #2)

(40 MINUTES RUNNING TIME)

CYCLE 2

(ENERGY BUMP UP ALL)

NICK—He is to remove poopy pants from himself . . . as if were where?
    His hearing finds no help from earrings or tattoos.
    Fuck you. He says "fuck you." The only tattoo that would have made
sense or dollars or doll hairs.
    Doll hairs needs trimming like baby brother's balls being bounced.
    Boing, boing, boing.
    Bye. Bye baby brother's balls.
    Be back before balls bloom on our friend guy. Bye bye buddy guy.
TERRI—*(separate words, separate thoughts—clarity of story)* I was mad
    when my sisters got sucked up. Now my brother. Something is sucking up
    my hugging family. Sherlock Holmes Rapper Super Lady must keep go-
    ing. . . . She's going to finger it out.
ANTHONY—Round and round we go. It's another twister.
TERRI—There's a clue in the dirt.
ANTHONY—Let's go find that twister.
TERRI—Super Lady will discover things violently. She will chase people while
    creeping. She will stay curious. She will fight.
ANTHONY—I can help you find what you're looking for.
TERRI—*(begins pacing, doubting herself)* I eat, I can jump, and hug at the
    same time. I am powerful, because I can fly. I can fly! I am different,
    because I can fight with my "business mind."

ANTHONY—Let's not pace.

TERRI—That's right I never pace.

ANTHONY—You're Sherlock Holmes Rapper Super Lady, remember?

NICK—It must have been a part of him, long before, because all it took was a soft breath in his ear. Less effort than the unthinkable, the automatic. To get that little part of him growing till it was him, or he was it, or either or rather.

Better you realize that small things can ruin the world or your world, or your big small world. All that surrounds the world, or all that surrounds an atom, or either or rather.

Maybe it's better if he doesn't remember his dreams.

Dreams stop the feeling for a moment. . . . Sorry.

ANTHONY—A to W at the speed of God. (snap fingers)

DENISE—You like speed.

NICK—I don't like limits.

LISA—But you do like David Hasselhoff.

TERRI—Another mess. The twister approached here.

ANTHONY—X Y Z before you blink your eyes.

SHARON—What do you want?

DENISE—No touchy. No touch no one.

This is a comparison: A feather is an S.O.S. pad in this world. (whisper)

NICK—Don't whisper.

LISA—Don't spit. Don't run. Don't shoot. Don't smoke.

DENISE—Listen kid, trip of Goats kid, no amigo Chico kid.

I can explained the rhythm of dirt.

SHARON—Your an old woman at 19 with an aged mind. She just toys with the idea of friendship.

DENISE—Sweaty man, sweaty boy, sweaty boy wants to feel like a sweaty man—is that it?

NICK—Your eyeballs full of red hots.

TERRI—Sweat surfaced on his vanilla skin.

NICK—(silent gulp of air)

CHARLES—Triggering senses and dealing with the consequences.

DENISE—Whoooo, slide your way down the memory.

LISA—Slide right over what you learned in Mr. Potts Algebra class. Wowoo!!!

TERRI—A young lion tears apart his fabric of reality.

ANTHONY—Was he in love?

TERRI—Listen to the rhythm.

CHAU—The only truth is in the alphabets. Can I play?

SHARON—Don't try and tell me about dedication, devotion, sincere undying love feeeeeelings that come from someplace so deep.

DENISE—Sit in it, sit. Climb through it. Chase it.

YUSUF—
>   Bow clear Paper hear
>   Wire pon pon threw.
>   Wait. Go Go. Wait Go.
>   Through it, run it,
>   Stick stick stick.
>   Rogeeea bow motions.
>   Push me—pull you.
>   Run it down.

NICK—Walls are hard. Windows are hard.
>   Especially when you're trying to penetrate.

SHARON—Try walking through those walls.

CHAU—A   B   C   D   E   F   G . . .

DENISE—I checked every wall for a soft spot. Now try the windows. Check every one. One, two . . . I'm going in search of two hearts.

SHARON—Let's go.

NICK—How the F can I leave. One hundred dependent souls depend on my sacred independence. This is something I learned on *Sesame Street*: "Today's show is sponsored by the letter F and the number zero to represent my tired life." *(closes eyes—body house)*

SHARON—Listen kid you don't touch her and you don't know where her ABC's have been.

DENISE—Can everyone say "Asshole" good boys and girls. Look at me.
>   Eyes all shut up. Face contorted like you're trapped in your "body house."

NICK—Maybe if I was someone else this would be easier. I heard the wind whisper to me that going naked might be my best disguise.

LISA—Maybe you didn't hear the wind correctly.

YUSUF—Crap. Snap. Tap . . . like toes pop ping pain . . . look over those? Who me? Can you feel, is it for real. . . . Someone steer the damn wheel . . .

SHARON—Go on move Faith to a new day.

DENISE—Forget the crap that they say, "believe in thy-self."

TERRI—Believe in self? Look under those leaves for more whispers.

ANTHONY—It's only two more people in search of two hearts.

SHARON—It was Honey marinated sperm that awakened her sleeping sex. Spotlights of lust and beds full of pain.
>   Cheddar cheese and buttered popcorn.
>   Sour patch kids and friendship bracelets.
>   Kids begging for macaroni.

NICK—
>   4 kids to a bed and roaches as pets
>   12 locks on the door and 3 knives under your mattress.

LISA—5 Playboys and a Miller Lite under your bed.

Lisa and Anthony—*(silent scream—trombone blast)*

Terri—His screams give her a little Jesus for a moment. It's twisted, but so is the sidewalk—so is a tree.

Anthony—A tree? A tree could be the shadow of this woman. Sherlock Holmes Crapper Stuper Baby. Woooo, I can fly. I'm creeping.

Terri—I can hear color. She's talking blue.

Chau—He's talking blue shit.

Denise—5,   10,   15,   20. I have a dime, a dime in my pocket. Rolling' around with a tantrum on my mind. . . .

Nick— . . . 5, 10, 15, 20 . . .

Denise—Triggering senses and dealing with the consequences.
    Clocks Tick Tock, Come on . . . make a decision? Crack Tick Tock, Crack Tick Clocks Tick Tock . . .

Yusuf—Tick Tock clack, Tick tock crack. Clocks tick tock.

Nick—I is olate? I is olate? Olate is? Is-olate. Isolated? . . . Isolated.

Denise—You're It. *(hand sticks to him)*

Anthony—Here's a note from the weather channel.

Terri—Touch down. Another twisted touchdown.

Nick—I twist. You twist. We twist.

INTERMISSION

(line up of actors . . . second line up
    Charles, Karen, Lisa—in band playing)

Sharon—Stop grabbing her pole like that—that must hurt. I'm sick of doing cartwheels with my hands becoming glued to the floor and my shirt falling over my head. I'm sick of hearing the word goody.

Yusuf—
    Buster clump pigeon vaulting.
    The glad sound of footsteps, wood creak easel, glandular easel.
    Poe-tops—tube socks.
    Button glut glob. It's the perch of the petulant queen.
    Sampson decay, Delilah slide away.
    Seamless backward detective work. Didn't do anything.

Terri—Like liquid flowing and stretching. It's all me. Maybe what I want to be and maybe what I am and will never be, but it's all me. I can be a river catching everything that is in my path, but I can also leave things behind. Baggage can only weigh one down and I want to move like a mind.

Chau—Chase it. Chase it. Run it down. *(write large letters in the air with punctuation)* That's all the truth you'll get from me.

Anthony—I haven't really figured it out, but I love to explore and to score big with ratings. I'm afraid of dating—I wish I wasn't. My cousin is a junking, sorry—Different subject. But the truth is—despite all my flaws, I'm pretty spunky.

NICK—Blink. Jump and stop. Blink. Smoothness stops. Blink. My eyes go blind. Blink. Eyes stop my sight. Blink. Even my heartbeat trips. Blink. My legs are yours. Blink my head is severed. Blink. I only see reflections, I cannot hear my breath. Follow follow I will swallow. Follow follow. I will try to follow your sight—I'll surrender my hindsight. Blink. Slow. Blink. Slow slow and be with me. Blink and open. Blink blink blink and breathe. Blink and breathe. Blink and breathe.

DENISE—I would like to act like a piece of wood that wants to light itself on fire.

(all walk to Big-E positions)

NICK—I twist. You twist, we twist.

DENISE—Whisper in my ear, sing me songs of love.

NICK—Ooh I'm digging you.

LISA—*(looks questioningly)*

DENISE—Snap your fingers. Fill all my dreams of you digging me.

NICK—Ohh I'm digging you.

LISA—*(looks questioningly)*

DENISE—Take me to a room of lust and lies, from all those other times. Rub your fingers down my . . .

NICK—Ohhh I'm digging you.

LISA—Rip the clothes off his body that his mama bought him. Tell him he's beautiful. Steal his innocence.

NICK—Damn she's digging me.

(1 minute—the Big-E breakdown)

TERRI—An earth quake breaks—stillness is found. There's just the breaths of a mountain or two. Right here.

   Stillness. This stillness was 8.2 on the Richter scale.

(AFTER SHOCK)

NICK—I . . . so . . . lated. I . . . so . . . lated. I . . . so . . . lated. He is isolated.

ANTHONY—I found pieces of people in trees, in the grass, in the river. There are times I hope you don't find what you're looking for.

NICK—Nothing more than thunder, darkness, clouds, this disrupt to heaven, man, woman. . . . Me.

TERRI—I want what happened here.

ANTHONY—Being here isn't enough.

TERRI—Always elsewhere! I keep dreaming Rapper Super Lady can't steer when she flies.

YUSUF—Steer the wheel.

ANTHONY—I'm the spare wheel.

TERRI—I want and want. I will figure things out with a bursting army of mind.

SHARON—Release, release. Kill her ass. Take her by the neck and squeeze until you break the bass and fall out the window.

NICK—No more cries leaking through the holes in my aching ears. I'm a brave heart searching for a piece of . . . A, B, C, D. . . . Mom, sister, brother, please hear me.

LISA—See me. Feel me. Touch me. Yada Yada Yada . . .

SHARON—I hear. At the edge of the sun there's a pool with a diving board and a juice bar. Jump. Plunge into emptiness with no daily appointments. . . . Just one big open call. That's a big dick of a headache going down.

ANTHONY—I don't want to play this game anymore. You want to go to a movie?

TERRI—What's wrong with you?

NICK—No touchy. No touch no one. This is a comparison: A feather was an S.O.S. pad in that world. *(whisper)*

SHARON—Don't whisper to me.

NICK—This won't rhyme or tell a story. This isn't something my Mama made me memorize to impress you.

DENISE—Triggering senses and dealing with the consequences are you?

CHAU—Next time won't you sing with me. *(sing with bass)*

NICK—She is many things, never could explain them to know one. I'm holding court four stories above a pretty thin book.

SHARON—Balance, you're short of it.

NICK—I understand. I really do understand the full movement of moving and the stillness of restriction.

LISA—You understand? You're a fucker filled with peanut butter and jelly.

TERRI—Blood rushes to my head with so little awareness that I'm in the middle of a thought. Where is it Watson?

ANTHONY—Love is a mystery. When it's solved I bet it vanishes.

NICK—Now I know my ABC's.

DENISE—5, 10, 15, 20. Still rolling around with a tantrum on my mind.

NICK—

Orange. Scary.

I'm a virgin—I've never done that.

Broken in—I. . . . hate . . . my . . . mom

(wave of people go across)

I hate band geeks. Cleaved lips.
"I want a boy friend with a nice car." "Not tonight I'm on the rag."
"You jerkoff!" Thank you.
I can't swim in this shit. I like all kinds of music.
Fuck softball.

(music breaks)

Brother. Shitty house.
"I don't need makeup." "Docile what?"
Shower? I don't look. I like motorcycles. Beer.
I don't want to be smart. I don't know.
I like McDonald's plates. I'll wreak your life.
I want a fast car too. Seat belts are for geeks.
Steel flowers.
DENISE—Maybe it's better if you don't remember your dreams.
NICK—
I am to remove poopy pants from myself . . . as if were where?
Here my hearing has been forced from my ears.
My hearing finds no help from earrings or tattoos.
Fuck you. I said "fuck you."
The only tattoo that would have made sense or cents or dollars or doll
   hairs.
Doll Hairs needs trimming like baby brother's balls being bounced.
Boing, boing, boing.
Bye. Bye baby brother's balls.
Be back before my balls bloom. Bye bye guy.
DENISE—Maybe if you were someone else this would be easier. Going
   naked might be your best disguise.
NICK—Listen kid, no amigo Chico kid. No touchy, no touch no one.
YUSUF—*(with all)*   Now, now, now, sound sound sound. Red red Face face
   face. No more . . . more. Redun. Redoune. Redone. Redone. Redundant.
NICK—With my pain all ablaze I turned to the left . . .
DENISE—A   B   C
CHARLES—*(Scale only . . .)*
TERRI—There's no more clues.
NICK—And I fell out of my world.

POSSESSION #2   *(MUSICIAN STAYS)*

(Nick finishes
1.   2 Antlines with Sharon and Anthony

2. *2nd Musician leaves*
3. *a group stillness is found—all holding notes riffing with music: 15 secs)*

ANTHONY—I'm the same old Watson! I never learn that the gravest issues depend on the smallest things. Buster clump pigeon vaulting! Watson. Watson. Watson.

(4. *all lead/all follow antline*
5. *Terri solo*
6. *Yusuf scat rap incorporated in the music*
7. *back wall that moves forward slides over to side wall*
8. *Yusuf finishes scat rap and Cycle 3 begins)*

CYCLE 3

YUSUF—He never pays attention to his body. He's wearing clean underwear. He's standing in a real cool position. He's not the originator. The originator is gone. He's got too many friends and he can't trust any them. He's got nice shoes. He's like . . . twisters and trains. Twisters and Trains hit him like a thought.

LISA—Look at me. Look at me. Eyes all shut up. Face contorted like you're trapped in your "body house." Knock. Knock.

YUSUF—Walls are hard. Windows are hard. Especially when you're trying to go through.

TERRI—I was mad when my sisters got sucked up. Then a brother. Now another brother. Sherlock Holmes Rapper Super Lady can't finger it out. I got no "business mind."

ANTHONY—Round and round and round we go. Let's go.

TERRI—How the F can I leave. One hundred dependent souls depend on Super Lady. This is something I learned on *Sesame Street*: "Today's show is sponsored by the letter F and the number zero to represent my tired life."

SHARON—
    It was Honey marinated sperm that awakened his sleeping sex.
    Spotlights of lust and beds full of pain.
    Cheddar cheese and buttered popcorn.
    Sour patch kids and friendship bracelets. Kids begging for macaroni.

ANTHONY—Here, hold my hand.

TERRI—No touchy. No touch no one. This is a comparison: A feather is an S.O.S. pad in Super Lady's world. *(whisper)*

ANTHONY—You don't have to whisper.

YUSUF—Dreams stop the feeling in my body for a moment.

LISA—Maybe it's better if you don't dream.

YUSUF—Tell me, are you it? Or should I twist with her? *(towards Terri who is falling into the twister)* Clocks tick tock, crack tick tock, come on make a decision. Crack tick tock . . .

CHARLES—Tick, tock, crack, tick tock crack.

SHARON—The only truth is in the Alpha—B.E.T.S.

TERRI—Touch down. A twister touched down right here.

SHARON—Release, release. Kill his ass. Take him by the neck and squeeze until you break the bass and fall out the window. Maybe if you two were someone else this would be easier.

YUSUF—Listen kid, no amigo Chico kid. No touchy, no touch no one.

CHARLES—Now, now, now, sound sound sound. Red red face face face. No more. . . . More. Redun. Redoune. Redone. Redone. Redundant.

YUSUF—With my pain all ablaze I turned to the left . . .

LISA—A   B   C

CHARLES—*(plays notes—A   B   C   D   E   F   G . . .)*

YUSUF—And I fell out of my world.

(MUSIC CHAOS: 20 count on—10 count off)

TERRI—Watson?

(10 count silence)

(BODY CHAOS ORDER OF MOVERS: Denise, Lisa, Terri, Yusuf, Anthony)

TERRI—Watson? *(bring instruments)* . . . Watson *(remove hats, Anthony, Nick, Sharon, Chau; Yusuf, Denise, Lisa bend down and touch floor)* . . . I saw an invisible man because he had a hat on. His hat blew off and that was the end of him . . . that I could see.

ANTHONY—That doesn't mean he isn't here.

TERRI—That was the disappearance of my faith in him.

YUSUF—It must have been a part of him, long before, because all it took was a soft breath in his ear. Less effort than the unthinkable, the automatic. Better you realize that small things can ruin the world or your world, or your big small world. All that surrounds the world, or all that surrounds an atom, or either or rather.

   Dreams stop the feeling in his body for a moment. He don't like that.

LISA—Sit in it, sit. Climb through it. Chase it.

SHARON—

   Bow clear Paper hear
   Wire pon pon threw.
   Wait. Go go. Wait go.

> Through it, run it,
> Stick stick stick.
> Rogeeea bow motions.
> Push me—pull you.
> Run it down.

TERRI—There is a speed limit and there are some people who attempt to travel at the speed of god.

LISA AND ANTHONY—You like speed.

YUSUF AND TERRI—I don't like limits.

YUSUF—No touchy. No touch no one. This isn't something my mama made me memorize to impress you.

SHARON—Someone steer the damn wheel . . .

ANTHONY—We are just two people, in search of two hearts.

TERRI—I am an invisible shape. It's defined quite well. . . . What it is composed of is unknown to man.

ANTHONY—Sounds like you just lost your hat.

TERRI—You can break down my elements, but in truth you cannot put my parts on a periodic table.

YUSUF—I twist. You twist. We twist.

ANTHONY AND YUSUF—Ohhhh I'm diggin' you.

ANTHONY—I dig you. I dig you. You are an environmental pain. Spanked by this drum. E . . . rup . . . t you Mother. Dru*m*s Dru*m*s—I like Dru*m*s.

NICK—Drug*s* Drug*s*—I like Dru*m*s.

(SLOW BIG E)

YUSUF—
I never pay attention to my body. I'm wearing clean underwear.
I'm standing in a real cool position.
I'm not the originator. The originator is gone.
The originator has left the building.
I've got too many friends and can't trust any of them. I've got nice shoes.
I like . . . twisters and trains.
Twisters and trains hit me like a thought.

(trombone train horn)

TERRI—I . . . wanted . . . to . . . move . . . like . . . a . . . mind . . . full . . . of . . . thoughts.

ANTHONY—An earthquake breaks—8.2 on the Richter scale.

CHARLES—*(plays the scale . . .)*

YUSUF—I . . . so . . . lated. I . . . so . . . lated. I . . . so . . . lated. He is isolated.

ANTHONY—I . . . so . . . lated. I . . . so . . . lated. I . . . so . . . lated. He is isolated.

TERRI—(aside) This is a monologue about great loss.

> She was Sherlock Holmes Rapper Super Lady.
> She always creeped to finger out what was sucking up her hugging family of friends.

> She discovered things violently.
> She would chase people while creeping.
> She was curious.
> She would eat, jump, and hug at the same time.
> She was powerful because she could fly.
> She was different because she could fight with her "business mind."
> She never paced. She never paced. She never paced.

> She was a child with long legs and small feet.
> She is 15 and 1/2 years old and doesn't like limits.
> She's caught.

ANTHONY—I was mad, I was really mad when Sherlock Holmes Super Rapper Lady got sucked up. I tried to finger out what was happening. I was creeping to finger out what sucked up my hugging friend.

> I found a clue in the dirt, Super Lady was sucked up, I believe . . . I know it was by a twister.

TERRI—It must have been a part of her, long before, because all it took was a soft breath in her ear. Less effort than the unthinkable, the automatic. To get that little part of her growing till it was her, or she was it, or either or rather.

> Better you realize that small things can ruin the world or your world, or your big small world.

> All that surrounds the world . . . or all that surrounds an atom . . . or either or rather.

(*Music builds like beginning, with Lisa circling behind. Terri stays alone and trembling in center of floor as music builds with single tones from everyone except—*

Anthony, who walks across stage left looking for clues. Grabs clue as final music cue.)

FINI

References

Arrastia, M., with Schwabacher, S., Betancourt, A., & Students of the Mothers' Reading Program. (1990). Community literature in the multi-cultural classroom: The mothers' reading program. In C. F. Walsh (Ed.), *Literacy as praxis: Culture, language, and pedagogy* (pp. 133–155). Norwood, NJ: Ablex.

Aylwin, S. (1985). *Structure in thought and feeling*. New York: Methuen.

Bakhtin, M. M. (1981). *The dialogic imagination: Four essays* (C. Emerson & M. Holquist, Trans.). Austin: University of Texas Press.

Bakhtin, M. M. (1986). *Speech genres & other late essays* (V. W. McGee, Trans.). Austin: University of Texas Press.

Bakhtin, M. M. (1990). *Art and answerability: Early philosophical essays* (V. Liapunov, Trans.). Austin: University of Texas Press.

Bakhtin, M. M. (1993). *Toward a philosophy of the act* (V. Liapunov, Trans.). Austin: University of Texas Press.

Bee, B. (1993). Critical literacy and the politics of gender. In C. Lankshear & P. McLaren (Eds.), *Critical literacy: Politics, praxis, and the postmodern* (pp. 101–122). Albany: State University of New York Press.

Bereiter, C., & Scardamalia, M. (1982). From conversation to composition. In R. Glaser (Ed.), *Advances in instructional psychology, Vol. 2*. Hillsdale, NJ: Erlbaum.

Britton, J. (1993). *Language and experience*. London: Penguin.

Brodkey, L. (1996). *Writing permitted in designated areas only*. Minneapolis: University of Minnesota Press.

Bruner, J. (1983). *Child's talk*. New York: Norton.

Bruner, J. (1986). *Actual minds, possible worlds*. Cambridge, MA: Harvard University Press.

Camitta, M. (1993). Vernacular writing: Varieties of literacy among Philadelphia high school students. In B. V. Street (Ed.), *Cross-cultural approaches to literacy* (pp. 228–246). New York: Cambridge University Press.

Chomsky, N. (1957). *Syntactical structures*. The Hague, the Netherlands: Mouton.

Cone, J. (1993a, Fall). Teaching the *Autobiography of Malcolm X*: The urgency of choice in an untracked classroom. *Teaching Tolerance Magazine*, 57–63.

Cone, J. (1993b). Using classroom talk to create community and learning. *English Journal, 82*, 30–38.

Cook-Gumperz, J. (1986). Literacy and schooling: An unchanging equation. In J. Cook-Gumperz (Ed.), *The social construction of literacy* (pp. 16–44). New York: Cambridge University.

Corbett, E. P. J. (1990). *Classical rhetoric for the modern student*. New York: Oxford University Press.

Doyle, A. C. (1917). The adventure of the second stain. In A. C. Doyle, *A treasure of Sherlock Holmes* (pp. 497–517). New York: International Collectors Library.

Duncan, G. (1996). Space, place, and the problematic of race: Black adolescent discourse as mediated action. *Journal of Negro Education, 65,* 133–150.

Dyson, A. H. (1989). *The multiple worlds of child writers: A study of friends learning to write.* New York: Teachers College Press.

Ellison, R. (1947/1990). *Invisible man.* New York: Vintage.

Emig, J. (1971). *The composing process of twelfth graders.* Urbana, IL: National Council of Teachers of English.

Fasheh, M. J. (1995). The reading campaign experience within Palestinian society: Innovative strategies for learning and building community. *Harvard Educational Review, 65,* 66–91.

Field, J. (Marion B. Milner, pseud.). (1937). *An experiment in leisure.* London: Virago.

Fleckenstein, K. S. (1996). Images, words, and narrative epistemology. *College English, 58,* 914–933.

Fox, R. (1994). Image studies: An interdisciplinary view. In R. Fox (Ed.), *Images in language, media, and mind* (pp. 3–20). Urbana, IL: National Council of Teachers of English.

Gee, J. (1990). *Social linguistics and literacies: Ideology in discourses.* New York: Falmer.

Gee, J. P., Hull, G., & Lankshear, C. (1996). *The new work order: Behind the language of the new capitalism.* Boulder, CO: Westview.

Glesne, C., & Peshkin, A. (1992). *Becoming qualitative researchers: An introduction.* White Plains, NY: Longman.

Graff, H. J. (1979). *The literacy myth: Literacy and social structure in the nineteenth-century city.* New York: Academic.

Griffith, M. (1982). *Writing to think.* Occasional Paper No. 4 of the National Writing Project, San Francisco.

Halliday, M. A. K. (1987). Spoken and written modes of meaning. In R. Horowitz & S. J. Samuels (Eds.), *Comprehending oral and written language* (pp. 55–82). San Diego: Academic.

Hartwell, P. (1985). Grammar, grammars, and the teaching of grammar. *College English, 47,* 105–127.

Hayes, J. R., & Flower, L. S. (1980a). Identifying the organization of writing processes. In L. W. Gregg & E. R. Steinberg (Eds.), *Cognitive processes in writing* (pp. 3–30). Hillsdale, NJ: Erlbaum.

Hayes, J. R., & Flower, L. S. (1980b). Writing as problem solving. *Visible Language, 14,* 388–399.

Henry, A. (1998, December). *Girls of African heritage: Examining literacy in two contexts.* Paper presented at the annual meeting of the National Reading Conference, Austin, TX.

Hillocks, G., Jr. (1986). *Research on written composition.* Urbana, IL: National Conference on Research in English.

Leont'ev, A. A. (1981a). The problem of activity in psychology. In J. V. Wertsch (Ed.), *The concept of activity in Soviet psychology* (pp. 37–71). New York: M. E. Sharpe.

Leont'ev, A. A. (1981b). Sign and activity. In J. V. Wertsch (Ed.), *The concept of activity in Soviet psychology* (pp. 241–255). New York: M. E. Sharpe.

Lindemann, E. (1995). *A rhetoric for writing teachers.* New York: Oxford University Press.

Lu, M.-Z. (1994). Professing multiculturalism: The politics of style in the contact zone. *College Composition and Communication, 45,* 442–458.

McCarthy, C. (1995). *The crossing.* New York: Vintage.

McLeod, A. (1986). Critical literacy: Taking control of our own lives. *Language Arts, 63,* 37–50.

Moffett, J. (1968). *Teaching the universe of discourse.* Boston: Houghton Mifflin.

Morson, G. S. (1996). *Narrative and freedom: The shadow of time.* New Haven, CT: Yale University Press.

New London Group. (1996). A pedagogy of multiliteracies: Designing social futures. *Harvard Educational Review, 66,* 60–92.

Paley, V. G. (1981). *Wally's stories.* Cambridge, MA: Harvard University Press.

Paley, V. G. (1990). *The boy who would be a helicopter: The use of story in the classroom.* Cambridge, MA: Harvard University Press.

Pianko, S. (1979). A description of the composing processes of college freshman writers. *Research in the Teaching of English, 13,* 5–22.

Rosenblatt, L. (1983). *Literature as exploration* (4th ed.). New York: Modern Language Association.

Rukeyser, M. (1978). *The collected poems.* New York: McGraw-Hill.

Schechner, R. (1985). *Between theater and anthropology.* Philadelphia, PA: University of Pennsylvania Press.

Scribner, S. (1984). Literacy in three metaphors. *American Journal of Education, 93,* 6–21.

Searle, D. (1984). Scaffolding: Who's building whose building? *Language Arts, 61,* 480–483.

Snow, C. (1983). Literacy and language: Relationships during the preschool years. *Harvard Educational Review, 53,* 165–189.

Stafford, B. M. (1997). *Good looking: Essays on the virtue of images.* Cambridge, MA: MIT Press.

Tompkins, J. (Ed.). (1980). *Reader-response criticism: From formalism to post-structuralism.* Baltimore, MD: Johns Hopkins University Press.

Turner, V. (1974). *Dramas, fields, and metaphors: Symbolic actions in human society.* Ithaca, NY: Cornell University Press.

Turner, V. (1986). *The anthropology of performance.* New York: Performing Arts Journal Publications.

Wertsch, J. V. (1991). *Voices of the mind: A sociocultural approach to mediated action.* Cambridge, MA: Harvard University Press.

Wilhelm, J. (1995). *"You gotta be the book."* New York and Urbana, IL: Teachers College Press and National Council of Teachers of English.

Wolf, S. A. (1994). Learning to act/acting to learn: Children as actors, critics, and characters in classroom theater. *Research in the Teaching of English, 28,* 7–44.

Wolf, S. A. (1996). Language in and around the dramatic curriculum. *Journal of Curriculum Studies, 27,* 117–137.

Zinchenko, V. P., & Gordon, V. M. (1981). Methodological problems in the psychological analysis of activity. In J. V. Wertsch (Ed.), *The concept of activity in Soviet psychology* (pp. 72–133). New York: M. E. Sharpe.

Index

About the Author

Christopher Worthman lives in Chicago and teaches literacy courses at DePaul University. He also facilitates critical literacy programs for teenage parents and continues to work with Free Street. Contact him at cworthma@depaul.edu.